OECD Development Co-operation Peer Reviews: Austria

2015

This work is published under the responsibility of the Secretary-General of the OECD. The opinions expressed and arguments employed herein do not necessarily reflect the official views of OECD member countries.

This document and any map included herein are without prejudice to the status of or sovereignty over any territory, to the delimitation of international frontiers and boundaries and to the name of any territory, city or area.

Please cite this publication as:
OECD (2015), *OECD Development Co-operation Peer Reviews: Austria 2015*, OECD Development Co-operation Peer Reviews, OECD Publishing.
http://dx.doi.org/10.1787/9789264227958-en

ISBN 978-92-64-22794-1 (print)
ISBN 978-92-64-22795-8 (PDF)

Series: OECD Development Co-operation Peer Reviews
ISSN 2309-7124 (print)
ISSN 2309-7132 (online)

The statistical data for Israel are supplied by and under the responsibility of the relevant Israeli authorities. The use of such data by the OECD is without prejudice to the status of the Golan Heights, East Jerusalem and Israeli settlements in the West Bank under the terms of international law.

Corrigenda to OECD publications may be found on line at: *www.oecd.org/about/publishing/corrigenda.htm*.

Conducting the peer review

The OECD's Development Assistance Committee (DAC) conducts periodic reviews of the individual development co-operation efforts of DAC members. The policies and programmes of each member are critically examined approximately once every four or five years. Five members are examined annually. The OECD's Development Co-operation Directorate provides analytical support, and develops and maintains, in close consultation with the Committee, the methodology and analytical framework – known as the Reference Guide – within which the peer reviews are undertaken.

The objectives of DAC peer reviews are to improve the quality and effectiveness of development co-operation policies and systems, and to promote good development partnerships for better impact on poverty reduction and sustainable development in developing countries. DAC peer reviews assess the performance of a given member, not just that of its development co-operation agency, and examine both policy and implementation. They take an integrated, system-wide perspective on the development co-operation and humanitarian assistance activities of the member under review.

The peer review is prepared by a team, consisting of representatives of the Secretariat working with officials from two DAC members who are designated as "examiners". The country under review provides a memorandum setting out the main developments in its policies and programmes. Then the Secretariat and the examiners visit the capital to interview officials, parliamentarians, as well as civil society and NGO representatives of the donor country to obtain a first-hand insight into current issues surrounding the development co-operation efforts of the member concerned. Field visits assess how members are implementing the major DAC policies, principles and concerns, and review operations in recipient countries, particularly with regard to poverty reduction, sustainability, gender equality and other aspects of participatory development, and local aid co-ordination. During the field visit, the team meets with representatives of the partner country's administration, parliamentarians, civil society and other development partners.

The Secretariat then prepares a draft report on the member's development co-operation which is the basis for the DAC review meeting at the OECD. At this meeting senior officials from the member under review respond to questions formulated by the Committee in association with the examiners.

This review contains the Main Findings and Recommendations of the Development Assistance Committee and the report of the Secretariat. It was prepared with examiners from Germany and Switzerland for the Peer Review of Austria on 3 December 2014.

Table of Contents

Tables

Figures

Boxes

Abbreviations and acronyms

ADA	Austrian Development Agency
ADC	Austrian Development Cooperation
ADF	African Development Fund
AfDB	African Development Bank
AsDB	Asian Development Bank
CGD	Center for Global Development
CODEV	EU Council Working Party on Development Cooperation
COHAFA	EU Council Working Group on Humanitarian Aid and Food Aid
CSO	Civil society organisation
DAC	Development Assistance Committee
DeREC	DAC Evaluation Resource Centre
EBRD	European Bank for Reconstruction and Development
EC	European Commission
ECOWAS	Economic Community of Western African States
EIB	European Investment Bank
EU	European Union
FAO	Food and Agriculture Organization of the United Nations
GDP	Gross domestic product
GHD	Good Humanitarian Donorship
GIZ	Deutsche Gesellschaft für Internationale Zusammenarbeit (German Federal Enterprise for International Cooperation)
GNI	Gross national income
HDI	Human Development Index
IaDB	Inter-American Development Bank
IASC	Inter-Agency Standing Committee
IBRD	International Bank for Reconstruction and Development
IDA	International Development Association
IFAD	International Fund for Agricultural Development
IFC	International Finance Corporation
IFI	International financial institution
IMF	International Monetary Fund
IUCN	International Union for Conservation of Nature
LDCs	Least developed countries
MDGs	Millennium Development Goals
MFA	Federal Ministry for Europe, Integration and Foreign Affairs
MIGA	Multilateral Investment Guarantee Agency

MoF	Federal Ministry of Finance
MOPAN	Multilateral Organisation Performance Assessment Network
NATO	North Atlantic Treaty Organization
NGO	Non-governmental organisation
OCHA	Office for the Coordination of Humanitarian Affairs (United Nations)
ODA	Official development assistance
OHCHR	Office of the High Commissioner for Human Rights (United Nations)
OSCE	Organization for Security and Co-operation in Europe
SDC	Swiss Agency for Development and Cooperation
Sida	Swedish International Development Cooperation Agency
TIKA	Turkish International Cooperation and Coordination Agency
UNAIDS	Joint United Nations Programme on HIV/AIDS
UNDP	United Nations Development Programme
UNFPA	United Nations Population Fund
UNICEF	United Nations Children's Fund

Signs used:

EUR	**Euro**
USD	**United States dollars**
( )	**Secretariat estimate in whole or part**
	(Nil)
0.0	**Negligible**
..	**Not available**
...	**Not available separately, but included in total**
n.a.	**Not applicable**

Slight discrepancies in totals are due to rounding.

Annual average exchange rate: 1 USD = EUR

2009	**2010**	**2011**	**2012**	**2013**
0.7181	0.7550	0.7192	0.7780	0.7532

Austria's aid at a glance

AUSTRIA

Net ODA	2011	2012	2013	Change 2012/13
Current (USD m)	1 111	1 106	1 172	6.0%
Constant (2012 USD m)	1 046	1 106	1 113	0.7%
In Euro (million)	799	860	882	2.6%
ODA/GNI	0.27%	0.28%	0.28%	
Bilateral share	44%	48%	46%	

Top Ten Recipients of Gross ODA (USD million)	
1 Côte d'Ivoire	50
2 Turkey	36
3 Bosnia and Herzegovina	27
4 China	19
5 Togo	16
6 Ukraine	12
7 Uganda	12
8 Kosovo	12
9 Serbia	11
10 Ethiopia	10
Memo: Share of gross bilateral ODA	
Top 5 recipients	28%
Top 10 recipients	40%
Top 20 recipients	53%

Gross Bilateral ODA, 2011-12 average, unless otherwise shown

Clockwise from top

By Income Group (USD m)

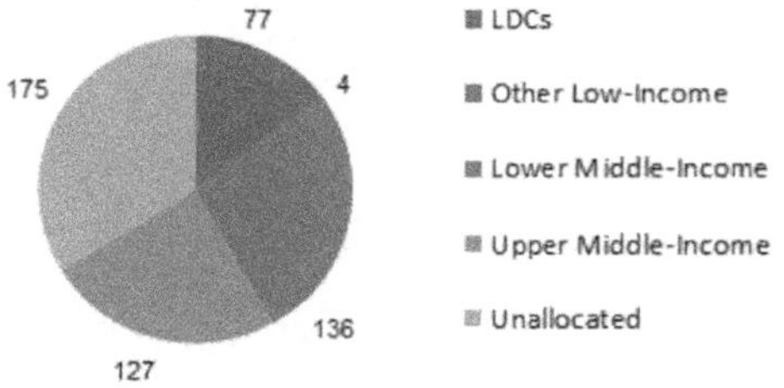

77
4
136
127
175
LDCs
Other Low-Income
Lower Middle-Income
Upper Middle-Income
Unallocated

By Region (USD m)

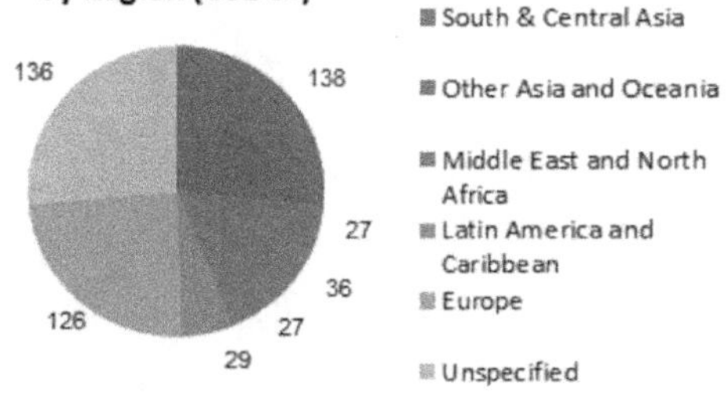

138
27
36
27
29
126
136
South of Sahara
South & Central Asia
Other Asia and Oceania
Middle East and North Africa
Latin America and Caribbean
Europe
Unspecified

By Sector

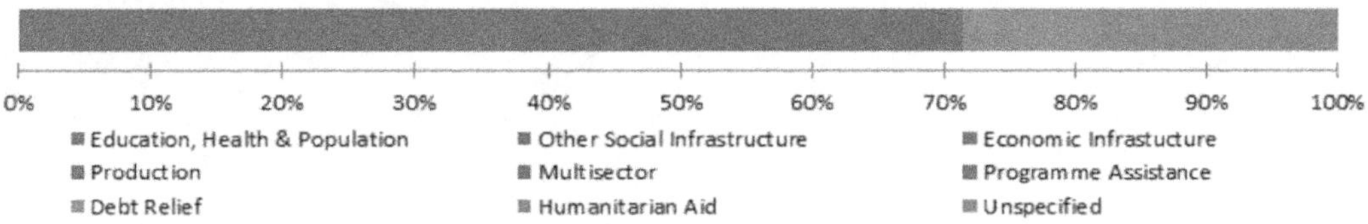

0%
10%
20%
30%
40%
50%
60%
70%
80%
90%
100%
Education, Health & Population
Other Social Infrastructure
Economic Infrastucture
Production
Multisector
Programme Assistance
Debt Relief
Humanitarian Aid
Unspecified

Source: OECD - DAC ; www.oecd.org/dac/stats

Figure 0.1 Austria's implementation of 2009 peer review recommendations

Implemented: 1
7%
Not implemented:
3
20%
Partially
implemented: 3
73%

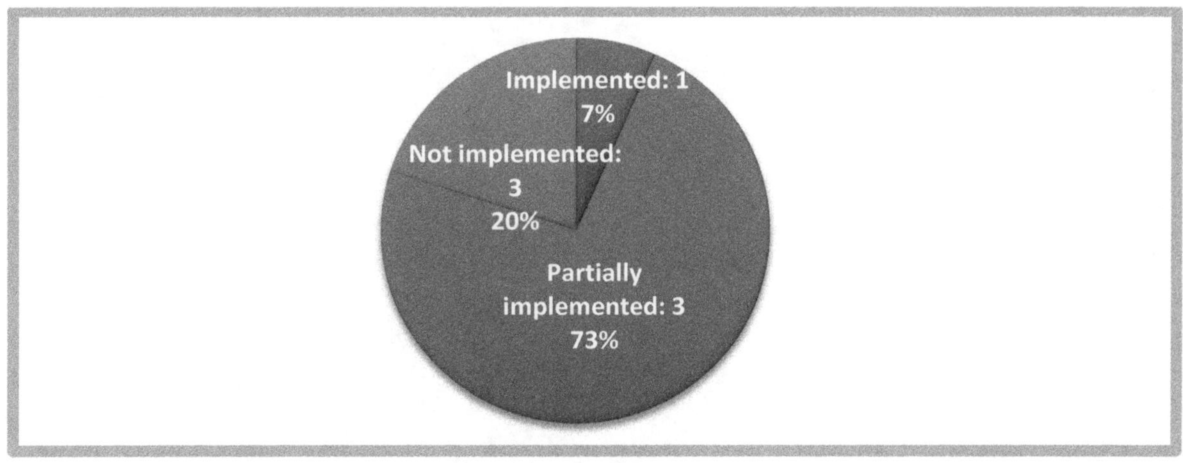

Context of Austria's Peer Review

Economic and political context

Austria is a prosperous and democratic country with a population of 8.5 million. It is a federal, parliamentary, democratic republic with nine states. The grand coalition government comprising the centre-left Social Democratic Party and the centre-right Austrian People's Party was renewed in December 2013 following the September general election to the National Council (*Naionalrat*). The two parties have a combined 99 seats in the 183-member National Council, providing a sense of political continuity and stability and keeping Austria firmly on a pro-European Union (EU) course. The next general election is scheduled to take place in 2018.

Austria, with its well-developed market economy, skilled labour force, and high standard of living, is closely tied to other EU economies, especially Germany's. Its economy features a large service sector, a sound industrial sector, and a small but highly developed agricultural sector. Following several years of solid demand for Austrian exports and record employment growth, the international financial crisis of 2008 and the subsequent global economic downturn led to a sharp but brief recession. Austrian GDP saw positive growth of about 2.9% in 2011, but growth fell to 0.7% in 2012 and 0.4% in 2013. According to the *OECD Economic Outlook*, Austria's GDP growth is set for a moderate but steady recovery – the OECD forecasts GDP growth to recover to 1.5% in 2014 and 2.1% in 2015 (OECD, 2014).

Unemployment did not rise as steeply in Austria as elsewhere in Europe, partly because the government subsidised reduced working hour schemes to allow companies to retain employees. Austria's fiscal position compares favourably with that of other euro zone countries, but it faces external risks, such as Austrian banks' continued exposure in Central and Eastern Europe, as well as political and economic uncertainties caused by the European sovereign debt crisis. In 2012 the budget deficit rose to 3.1% of GDP. In March of the same year, the Austrian parliament approved an austerity package consisting of a mix of expenditure cuts and new revenues that will bring public finances into balance by 2016. As this peer review report shows, austerity measures have also significantly affected the levels of Austria's development assistance.

The *OECD Economic Outlook* states: "On the downside, events in Ukraine, with potential knock-on effects to other Central and Eastern European countries, could harm export growth and the financial sector. Although recent measures to strengthen the capital position of banks were effective, the asset quality review and stress test may reveal additional capital needs. This could lead to reductions in bank assets. On the upside, a stronger-than-projected recovery in Austria's trading partners and a quicker restoration of confidence in the wake of further progress on the euro-area banking union could lead to a stronger pick-up of exports and domestic demand" (OECD, 2014).

Since the 2009 DAC peer review, the Austrian federal government has been trying to focus its support on fewer countries and thematic areas. Austria views development co-operation as an important aspect of foreign policy for "strengthening international solidarity" (GoA, 2013) and to address global challenges (MFA, 2012). This peer review looks at Austria's efforts since 2009 to increase the impact of its aid and the efficiency of its distribution.

Sources:

EIU (Economist Intelligence Unit) (2014), "Austria", March 2014, EIU, London, http://country.eiu.com/austria.

GoA (Federal Government of Austria) (2013), *Work Programme of the Austrian Federal Government 2013-2018*: *Austria*, Austrian Federal Chancellery, Vienna, www.bka.gv.at/DocView.axd?CobId=53588.

MFA (Federal Ministry for Europe, Integration and Foreign Affairs) (2012), Three Year Programme on Austrian Development Policy 2013-2015, MFA, Vienna, www.entwicklung.at/uploads/media/ThreeYearProgramme_13-15_02.pdf.

OECD (2014), OECD *Economic Outlook*, Vol. 2014/1, OECD Publishing, Paris, http://dx.doi.org/10.1787/eco_outlook-v2014-1-en.

OECD (2013), *OECD Economic Surveys*: Austria 2013, OECD Publishing, Paris, http://dx.doi.org/10.1787/eco_surveys-aut-2013-en.

The DAC's main findings and recommendations

1. Towards a comprehensive Austrian development effort

Indicator: The member has a broad, strategic approach to development and financing for development beyond aid. This is reflected in overall policies, co-ordination within its government system, and operations.

Main Findings

Austria effectively engages in the international development landscape, and delivers on its commitment to addressing global public risks and processes that affect development. The government's strategy takes a realistic approach, focusing on a few policy areas, such as the rule of law, human rights, peace and security, where it believes it can add value. For example, Austria makes an important contribution to tackling global and regional security challenges through its active participation in United Nations (UN) and European Union (EU) peacekeeping operations around the world. Its "perpetual neutrality" – a core element of Austrian foreign policy – reinforces its international role as a mediator, enabling it to carry its weight and enhance its influence at the global level.

At home, Austria is working to make its policies more development friendly and coherent. Policy coherence for development is an explicit objective in the government's Work Programme 2013-2018 and has guided Austria in the elaboration of its national positions on the post-2015 development agenda. Moreover, in keeping with the EU framework on policy coherence for development, Austria has identified the environment and security as its priority objectives for policy coherence, supported by cross-ministerial strategic guidelines endorsed by the Cabinet. During the review, Austria mentioned that the ongoing evaluation of the strategic guidelines on environment and development offers an opportunity to reinforce a coherent approach to climate finance and finance for development.

Ensuring that development concerns are better understood and discussed across the federal government is challenging, however. While the Federal Act on Development Co-operation provides the legal basis for the Federal Ministry for Europe, Integration and Foreign Affairs (MFA) to act as the main conduit for ensuring policy coherence for development, in reality, clear procedures, mechanisms and adequate human resources are not in place for the ministry to fulfil this role effectively. There also remains a general perception among federal ministries that policy coherence for development is only about co-ordinating development co-operation policy and interventions. The MFA acknowledges the need to improve awareness within the federal government of the impact of Austria's non-ODA policies on the development prospects of its partner countries.

Furthermore, Austria does not have a clear approach to addressing policy incoherence. This prevents Austria from fully translating its political commitment to policy coherence for development into practice and actual policy changes. Like many OECD Development Assistance Committee (DAC) members, Austria lacks the institutional mechanisms or capacity to measure, monitor, analyse and report the impact of its domestic and foreign policies on development. The existing expertise and analytical capacity found in Austrian think tanks and non-governmental organisations (NGOs) are also not yet exploited fully to gather sound evidence on coherence issues.

Austria recognises the importance of using innovative financing as a means to broaden its approach to international development. Austria's desire to deepen private sector engagement in development co-operation is clearly reflected in its increased emphasis on using ODA as a catalyst to leverage private finance. However, its objectives and expected results linked to development effectiveness are not well defined. How Austria ensures that its private sector activities and instruments contribute to poverty reduction outcomes, is unclear. The committee was informed that Austria is preparing interministerial guidelines on private sector development which provides an opportunity to address this concern.

Since the last peer review, Austria has raised substantial amounts of non-ODA funds in addition to its traditional ODA engagement through its small but fast-growing development finance institution, the Austrian Development Bank. Building on this, the Austrian Development Agency (ADA) and the Bank are encouraged to deepen their partnership and look for more positive synergies to achieve greater development impact.

Recommendations

1.1. Austria should develop a clear approach to addressing policy incoherence, prioritising selected topics and mechanisms and including means of monitoring and reporting across government, while drawing on the expertise and analytical capacity existing in the country.

1.2. To ensure development effectiveness, Austria needs to set out clear developmental objectives and expected results of using ODA as a catalyst to leverage private investment.

2. Austria's vision and policies for development co-operation

Indicator: Clear political directives, policies and strategies shape the member's development co-operation and are in line with international commitments and guidance.

Main Findings

The mission statement which is included in Austria's Three-Year Programme 2013-2015 identifies the overall purpose and main priorities of Austrian Development Cooperation (ADC) and has wide ownership. The 2003 Federal Act on Development Co-operation and the Three-Year Programme provide the legal and strategic focus for Austria's ODA programme, with poverty reduction at the centre. The Three-Year Programme is more strategic and result-oriented than previous rolling triennial programmes. However, it does not cover all the aid-spending federal ministries. Bringing these ministries in line with, and making them accountable for achieving the objectives of the three-year programmes would contribute to improving the coherence and effectiveness of Austria's development co-operation.

The Three-Year Programme 2013-2015 notes that the least-developed countries, European neighbours and fragile states are at the heart of Austria's approach to development co-operation. However, it does not provide a sufficient rationale for allocating resources to these countries and regions, and to the different channels and instruments of Austrian aid. Allocation criteria are necessary to safeguard aid predictability for partners and Austrian actors. Austria's approach to the EU focuses on implementing and influencing the EU's development agenda. Its approach to the international financial institutions shows a clear profile, but is less strategic as concerns the UN organisations. Funding to these organisations has become unpredictable, mostly as a result of decreases in Austrian ODA.

Austria's development co-operation covers a wide range of sectors and themes relative to its limited ODA resources. It is committed to focusing on two to three sectors in each priority country and has elaborated strategic documents for most of its priority sectors and themes. A number of strategies could better reflect the changing global context and Austria's funding realities. When revising these documents, Austria needs to be realistic about what it can achieve and to focus on areas where it can add value. Linking the priorities for reducing poverty to result-oriented methodologies and tools for reporting and learning would be useful.

Austria's guidance on working in fragile contexts has increased dialogue on these issues within government. It reports that all its programmes in fragile states take into account its peacebuilding and statebuilding goals. How this is done in practice is not entirely clear. Although Austria's funding to NGOs can be multi-annual and thus can allow them to incorporate recovery elements as the context evolves, there are no formal links between humanitarian and development programmes, including in priority countries.

The security and development guideline seeks to achieve a comprehensive, whole-of-government approach to human security, recognising the centrality of the Fragile States Principles. The planned review of this guideline could provide a useful opportunity for Austria to reinforce its political commitments to addressing fragility, and to develop a strategy for designing programmes with a fragility lens.

Mainstreaming gender and the environment throughout Austria's development co-operation continues to be work-in-progress. The share of its bilateral aid targeting these topics has been falling in recent years, and is well below the DAC average. Given its limited ODA resources, Austria is encouraged to clarify its priorities for mainstreaming cross-cutting themes throughout its development co-operation, and to ensure that it has the tools and resources to follow through on these priorities.

Recommendations

2.1. Austria should bring all aid-spending ministries in line with, and make them accountable for, achieving the objectives of the three-year programmes.

2.2. Having a clear rationale for allocating resources geographically, by channel and by instrument, would increase the predictability of Austrian aid.

2.3. Austria is encouraged to clarify its priorities for mainstreaming cross-cutting themes, and to ensure that it has the tools and resources to follow through on these priorities.

3. Allocating Austria's development assistance

Indicator: The member's international and national commitments drive aid volume and allocations.

Main Findings

In 2013 Austria's net ODA amounted to USD 1.2 billion, the equivalent of 0.28% of its gross national income (GNI). Its aid levels declined substantially in 2009, mostly as a result of the drop in debt relief, which was exceptionally high between 2005 and 2008. The decrease in debt relief posed some challenges for the government in regard to coming up with fresh resources for aid. Nevertheless, Austria has managed to keep its ODA volume relatively stable.

The Austrian authorities remain committed at the highest level to providing 0.7% of GNI as ODA. Their intention to develop a legally binding roadmap to achieve this target is therefore a positive step. However, the review team has learned that cuts in the ODA budget are foreseen in 2015 and beyond. How Austria will deliver on its ODA commitment without safeguarding the budget from further cuts is uncertain.

The share of Austria's bilateral aid that is programmed at country level remains small. In 2012 that share reached only 15% of Austria's total bilateral aid, far below the DAC average of 55%. A low level of country programmable aid means Austria is limited in what it can aspire to as a bilateral donor. For instance, even though most of Austria's country programmable aid targets its 11 priority countries and territories, the share of Austrian aid to these countries and territories represented only 14% of its total bilateral aid in 2012. Therefore, Austria's priority partner countries and territories do not figure prominently among the overall top Austrian aid recipients. Equally, even though nearly 45% of its country programmable aid goes to the least-developed countries (LDCs), Austria's stated poverty focus is challenged by the drop in its gross bilateral ODA to LDCs, excluding debt relief, since the last review.

Contrary to the 2009 peer review recommendation, Austria continues to rely on debt relief as a significant component for meeting its ODA commitments. It has forecast its 2013-15 bilateral ODA budget based on expected debt cancellations. However, the inclusion of debt relief before this has been agreed by the Paris Club is not practised by any other DAC member. Doing so inflates projections and undermines Austria's credibility and the predictability of its future aid flows. The failed Paris Club negotiations between Sudan and its creditors in 2012 have demonstrated the risk in using over-optimistic forecasts.

OECD data show that Austria supported an average of six sectors in its main partner countries in 2012. Austria's "nexus approach" to implementing its thematic priorities often requires a multi-sector approach to be effective, giving the impression that its aid portfolio is fragmented. Nevertheless, Austria's overall sectoral allocations appear to reflect its policy priorities, with nearly 60% of its bilateral ODA (USD 339 million) allocated to social infrastructure and services in 2011-12. A large part of that amount was spent on education (including imputed student costs) followed by health. Support to economic infrastructure has also been increasing over the years.

Austria mostly provides core funding to its multilateral partners and is committed to increase this funding further. The EU alone receives a quarter of Austria's total ODA, while another quarter goes to international financial institutions. It also actively contributes to the governing boards of these institutions. Austrian funds provided to the UN organisations have declined in recent years, mostly affecting core contributions. For Austria to engage with its multilateral partners with a long-term perspective, it will need to ensure predictability in its contributions to the UN organisations over the medium-term.

Recommendations

3.1. Austria should deliver on its commitment to develop a realistic time-bound roadmap to increase ODA in order to make progress towards meeting the 0.7% ODA/GNI target.

3.2. Austria should include debt relief in its ODA forecasts only after this is agreed by the Paris Club.

3.3. Austria should reverse the decline in the share of its ODA allocated to the LDCs, in keeping with its commitment to poverty reduction.

4. Managing Austria's development co-operation

Indicator: The member's approach to how it organises and manages its development co-operation is fit for purpose.

Main Findings

As there are nine government institutions involved in Austrian aid, managing the system efficiently around the objectives of the three-year programmes requires strong political will, as well as buy-in from the relevant federal ministries. The MFA has overall responsibility for Austria's development co-operation, including co-ordinating and formulating policy, overseeing ADA's operational and administrative budget, and representing Austria in relevant EU committees. However, the ministry directly manages less than 5% of total ODA and has no formal authority over the other federal ministries, which operate independently with separate mandates and discretionary budgets. This makes the MFA's co-ordinating role a challenging task.

The Austrian Development Agency (ADA) implements development programmes together with other public institutions, NGOs and private enterprises. Its operational budget has shrunk significantly, from EUR 103 million in 2008 to EUR 66 million in 2012. The budget was stabilised in 2013 and 2014 despite expected cuts. Further cuts were planned in 2015 and beyond but the Committee was informed that no cuts are expected in 2015. The uncertainty of funding makes the agency's financial planning and programming difficult. By implementing EU-financed projects with other development partners, ADA is able to increase the volume of aid which it manages and retain technical expertise. This complies with the EU Agenda for Change and its business plan. At the same time, that approach puts ADA in a competitive position with respect to other European development agencies, making its resource base less predictable. This could put at risk the agency's ability to implement the official aid programme effectively.

Austria has vested a substantial amount of decision-making authority in the country offices since the last peer review. In Moldova the joint representation of the MFA and ADA, under the strategic leadership of the head of Austrian Development Cooperation (ADC), strengthens the visibility and role of ADC, facilitates interactions between these entities and with the partner country, and reduces the layers and levels of project approval. However, there is no formalised system for bringing the other federal ministries in line around ADC's country strategy, and ADC's head does not have the authority to do this. Thus the effectiveness of Austria's aid at country level is not maximised.

Managing human resources efficiently within ADC remains challenging. The number of development experts in the MFA is expected to decrease, with several retirements upcoming and no plans to replace them. Staff exchanges and rotations with other organisations, including federal ministries, are rare. Recognising development co-operation as a career path within the ministry, and ensuring that the right skills are in the right places, including for dealing with fragile contexts, would be important steps forward. For its part, ADA has experienced staff reductions since the last peer review and is vulnerable to additional budget cuts. It does not sufficiently prioritise staff training and institutional learning. By contrast, the Austrian Development Bank's growing activities have led to the recruitment of new staff, and staff numbers at the Federal Ministry of Finance working on the aid programme have remained stable.

The follow-up to the post-2015 sustainable development agenda will offer Austria an opportunity to review the range of competencies needed to address the development challenges linked to that agenda, review the division of labour among the different institutions involved, and increase the coherence of the entire aid system with a view to improving the delivery of Austrian aid. An important step towards a more unified approach would be for the federal ministries, ADA and the Bank, when involved in the same priority partner countries, to agree on a set of common development objectives so that these countries can fully capitalise on the range of Austria's competencies. Drawing on the experiences of other DAC members, including Switzerland's, might be useful in this context. ADA and the Bank, in particular, are well placed to build strong linkages across their respective programmes and combine their activities to meet the development priorities of Austria's partner countries.

Recommendations

4.1. Austria should ensure that, when involved in the same priority countries, the federal ministries, ADA and the Austrian Development Bank agree on a set of common development objectives, elaborate joint country strategies, and report on a single set of country results.

4.2. Austria needs to develop a staff development strategy to ensure that it has the competence and expertise to engage in and deliver quality aid in its priority partner countries.

5. Austria's development co-operation delivery and partnership

Indicator: The member's approach to how it delivers its programme leads to quality assistance in partner countries, maximising the impact of its support, as defined by Busan.

Main Findings

Austria has worked to make its development co-operation more predictable since the last peer review. Its multi-year ODA forecast is updated annually in line with the rolling four-year national budget framework. Aid predictability at country level remains partial, however. Austria formally communicates indicative spending plans to only three of its priority countries. Providing similar information consistently to all priority countries would enhance these countries' ability to plan.

Austria's support is aligned to partner countries' strategies and draws upon its own experience. As the review team observed in Moldova, Austria identifies projects in close consultation with its local partners. This has helped ensure alignment.

Austria also actively supports and engages in donor co-ordination in the field. Moreover, it actively supports the EU Code of Conduct on the Division of Labour. The programme in Moldova clearly demonstrates Austria's ability to identify opportunities for delegated co-operation in line with the EU Agenda for Change.

While Austria is making some progress in implementing the aid effectiveness principles, project-based assistance continues to be its preferred approach for delivering aid, and country systems are not used by default. Where these systems are not robust, working together with the partner government and other external stakeholders to strengthening them would allow Austria to support the long-term development of partner country capacities.

Fiduciary risk is analysed in Austria's development co-operation. However, how major risks to the success of its overall development portfolio are identified, analysed, managed or monitored is not clear. For instance, while the country office in Moldova takes a systematic approach to risks in its activities in the breakaway region of Transnistria, its staff are left to decide the best ways to incorporate risk management into programming, thus possibly exposing the overall aid portfolio, and Austria's aid institutions, to significant unmanaged threats.

Austria's untying performance has been well below the DAC average. With respect to ODA covered by the DAC Untying Recommendation, the share of untied aid fell from 95% in 2010 to 77% in 2012, well below the DAC average of 88%. Overall untying of Austria's total bilateral ODA fell even more dramatically, from 58% to 37% over the same period. These changes are a result of a reduction of bilateral ODA. In contrast, the DAC average (78% in 2012) has held up well since Accra despite the global economic and financial crisis.

NGOs are important development partners of the Austrian aid programme. However, Austria's approach for engaging with civil society in partner countries does not appear strategic. Clear engagement policy or objectives at both strategic and delivery levels are needed.

Austria is committed to the Fragile States Principles, but does not yet consistently apply a fragility lens for programming in these complex and constantly changing contexts. Reducing the scope of its priorities for peacebuilding and statebuilding in order to be more realistic could be a useful next step. Partnership with civil society actors in fragile contexts is good practice, given that most fragility programmes are delivered through partners and multi-donor trust funds. Austria also makes a significant contribution to peacebuilding efforts.

Recommendations

5.1. Austria is encouraged to introduce a more comprehensive and systematic approach to risk management in its development co-operation programme, including at partner country level.

5.2. Austria should reverse the decline in the share of its aid that is untied, bearing in mind the Accra and Busan commitments.

5.3. Austria should engage more strategically with civil society in the countries where it works, based on clear guidelines.

5.4. Austria should consistently apply a fragility lens to programming in fragile states.

6. Results management and accountability of Austria's development co-operation

Indicator: The member plans and manages for results, learning, transparency and accountability.

Main Findings

Austria has taken a number of important steps in favour of managing for results since the last peer review. These include annexing a results matrix to the Three-Year Programme, with expected outcomes for the sectors and themes of Austria's priority countries and regions; introducing results management approaches in NGO funding guidelines, applications and reporting; and dedicated training and experience-sharing workshops for staff at headquarters and at field level. Austrian Development Cooperation (ADC) has also begun to use country data and national monitoring frameworks in a number of priority countries, and the new format of country strategies comprises output and outcome indicators aligned with the national priorities. These practices need to be systematised as Austria further develops results frameworks for all its country programmes. For its part, the Federal Ministry of Finance requires project-specific results frameworks in multi-bi programmes, and the Austrian Development Bank measures results using a rigorous and comprehensive framework.

While these efforts are significant, Austria still lacks a consistent and coherent approach to development results, as well as a system to inform programming decisions and serve accountability needs. Developing a differentiated approach to setting out, monitoring and reporting expected results in fragile contexts, and ensuring that this approach supports learning and accountability, also remains to be done.

Austria has made good progress with respect to evaluation. The management response system for strategic evaluations is a welcome initiative. The next step is to get senior managers to ensure that the findings are acted upon, so that evaluations effectively inform strategic decisions and are used as a management tool. Setting up an evaluation committee under an independent oversight body would contribute to increasing commitment at all levels to follow up on recommendations from evaluations. Austria includes national experts in project evaluation teams and is encouraged to support country-led efforts in this area.

The culture of sharing knowledge and the system for managing knowledge are still weak within ADC. ADA's new knowledge management strategy, dedicated core team and action plan are important steps towards a more structured and institutionalised system. At this stage, however, efforts have focused primarily on elaborating rules for managing knowledge assets and integrating knowledge goals into ADA's business plan. As observed in Moldova, the resources for organising and capitalising on project information at field level are insufficient, and experience sharing is therefore limited. The lack of updated technology and systems for managing information appears to constitute a bottleneck.

Austria has published an implementation schedule for the common and open standard for electronic publication of development co-operation resources. It performs well on sharing organisation-level information, but does not sufficiently communicate on development results and risks. Improving domestic accountability is also challenging. The MFA may want to reflect strategically on how to sensitise parliamentarians more and ensure that they are informed about development results achieved.

Austria's approach to communication and development education has been reinforced with a strategy and dedicated budgets. Austria works with civil society actors to raise development awareness. Supporting domestic advocacy NGOs, and reaching out to civil society beyond the traditional Austrian actors, could stimulate a broader public debate on development within Austria.

Recommendations

6.1. Austria is encouraged to develop a consistent and coherent approach to development results as well as a system to inform programming decisions and serve accountability needs.

6.2. Setting up an evaluation committee under an independent oversight body would contribute to increasing commitment at all levels to follow up on recommendations from evaluations.

6.3. Having a more strategic approach to communicating about development results and risks, and increasing transparency on how ADC is working, would contribute to promoting a culture that is more open to public information.

7. Austria's humanitarian assistance

Indicator: The member contributes to minimising the impact of shocks and crises; and saves lives, alleviates suffering and maintains human dignity in crisis and disaster settings.

Main Findings

Austria has a strong historical involvement with some themes of humanitarian assistance, especially the protection of civilians and human rights. There is also a commitment to support the "self-help capacities" of vulnerable populations; this is mostly done through the World Bank's risk reduction facility. Civil-military co-ordination is also a focus for Austria, including training its own peacekeeping troops and those of the Economic Community of Western African States (ECOWAS), in an effort to enlarge humanitarian space.

There are good practices in the programme; Austria can provide multi-annual funding to NGO partners, allowing them to adapt programmes to evolving recovery contexts, partners report good relationships with Austrian humanitarian staff, and information about the humanitarian programme is made public.

However, there is significant fragmentation in Austria's humanitarian system. Reflection on cross-governmental co-ordination is encouraged, so that Austria can make the most of its humanitarian resources and expertise to forge more effective humanitarian results. In addition, Austria does not yet have clear funding allocation criteria, applicable across government and based on its comparative advantage. This makes it difficult to deliver consistent and measurable results across the fragmented programme, and decreases predictability for partners. Moreover, funding from the Foreign Disaster Relief Fund is determined by the Council of Ministers, potentially a risk to the apolitical and principled nature of humanitarian assistance, as well as a rather slow process in practice. In addition, many grants and bilateral interventions are very small; these grants could be scaled up or consolidated to increase efficiency.

Austria's funding to multilateral agencies is only lightly earmarked; this is good practice. However, allocations fluctuate significantly and must be renegotiated each year, hampering predictability. This also contributes to a high administrative burden for Austria's partners. In addition, the timeliness of disbursements for new and escalating crises is an issue; here Austria relies on its civil protection deployments, which are much quicker than providing funding to partners. Partner activities and results are monitored, mostly through reports, dialogue and field visits, but this is difficult when Austria provides funding for so many different crises.

The evaluation of Austria's humanitarian aid in 2010 was useful, but most recommendations were not implemented. The management response indicated that this was due to the lack of volume and predictability of the humanitarian budget; however the recommendations on strategy, reducing fragmentation, and improving monitoring could have been taken on board. Monitoring of Austria's on-going performance as a humanitarian donor is complicated, as it has not yet set verifiable indicators for the cross-government programme.

Finally, Austria allocated 3.3% of its total ODA to its own humanitarian assistance programme in 2012, a smaller share than would be expected from a DAC member. Sixty percent was provided as assessed contributions to the EU, leaving Austria with only USD 18.1 million for its own humanitarian efforts. These limited financial resources do not allow Austria to play a "distinctive role." Austria has made a political commitment to allocate EUR 20 million per year to the Foreign Disaster Response Fund, compared to the current EUR 5 million; however, this has not yet become reality, despite broad cross-party support.

Recommendations

7.1. Austria should reflect on its humanitarian achievements, and develop a strategic focus and allocation criteria for its humanitarian programme, in order to increase predictability, facilitate performance monitoring, and to raise its profile on the international stage.

7.2. Commitments to scale up the humanitarian budget should be kept, so that Austria can match its strategic ambitions with adequate resources.

Secretariat's report

Chapter 1: Towards a comprehensive Austrian development effort

Global development issues

Austria contributes strategically to addressing global public risks and processes that affect development. Its strategy focuses on a few thematic issues such as human rights, peace and security, where it believes it can add value and exert influence on the global stage. Austria's commitment to tackle critical and challenging global development issues is commendable.

Austria makes a focused and strategic contribution to global development

Austria considers "establishing a regulated and equitable world order" through effective collective action to be in its own interest (GoA, 2013). It uses both bilateral relations and EU instruments to contribute strategically to addressing global public risks and to processes that are important for Austria and Europe. Its strategy, as set out in the government's Work Programme 2013-2018 (GoA, 2013), focuses on a few policy areas where it believes it can make an impact, such as the rule of law, human rights, peace and security, all of which lie at the heart of its foreign policy and are in line with the EU Agenda for Change.

Austria makes an important contribution to tackling global security challenges. Preventing conflicts and promoting peace are high on its list of priorities. For example, Austria:

- plays an active role in the Organization for Security and Co-operation in Europe (OSCE), including hosting the OSCE Secretariat in Vienna.
- although not a North Atlantic Treaty Organization (NATO) member, participates in NATO-led initiatives, such as the Partnership for Peace and the International Security Assistance Force in Afghanistan.
- deploys military personnel to a number of UN and EU peacekeeping operations around the world (784 across 15 countries and regions as of March 2014).
- is a leading provider of peacekeeping training.

Austria's Vienna 3C Appeal (GoA et al., 2010; Box 1.1) provides the whole-of-government framework for engagement in the security sector. Moreover, its "perpetual neutrality" – a core element of its foreign policy – reinforces its international role as a mediator and enables it to enhance its influence at the global level (e.g. by hosting the 5+2 negotiations on Transnistria in Vienna).

Austria's foreign policy, including its development policy, is also strongly directed towards Central and Eastern Europe. Focusing on ensuring security in the region, Austria actively plays a "bridging" role and promotes regional co-operation and exchange of experience on European integration between EU and non-EU Central and Eastern European states through the Central European Initiative, which it co-founded, and in the framework of the European Neighbourhood Policy.

Policy coherence for development

Indicator: Domestic policies support or do not harm developing countries

Austria remains committed to policy coherence for development, at both the national and EU levels. While it has made progress since the last peer review, it can go further. Austria lacks a clear approach to addressing policy incoherence, including means of monitoring and reporting across government. It could build on its good practice in the areas of environment and security to better engage the public in promoting policy coherence for development. Austria could also exploit the expertise and analytical capacity found in think tanks and non-governmental organisations (NGOs) to gather sound evidence to underpin inter-ministerial discussions on coherence issues.

Austria is committed to making its policies more development friendly, but needs a more systematic approach to ensure policy coherence for development across government

Austria has endorsed the OECD Ministerial Declaration on Policy Coherence for Development (OECD, 2008). Its commitment to development friendly and coherent policies, at both the national and EU levels, is clearly referred to in the Federal Act on Development Co-operation and is at the core of the Three-Year Programme on Austrian Development Policy 2013-2015.[1] Policy coherence for development is also an explicit objective in the government's Work Programme 2013-2018. Austria's commitment to policy coherence is well illustrated by its efforts to ensure coherent national positions on the post-2015 development agenda through an inclusive process, widely consulting various government and civil society actors (OECD, 2014).

In keeping with the EU framework on policy coherence for development (EU, 2009), Austria has defined the environment and security as its specific objectives for policy coherence, supported by cross-ministerial strategic guidelines endorsed by the Cabinet. The guidelines establish cross-governmental objectives that are agreed to and owned by relevant ministries, although a time-bound plan for achieving these objectives is still lacking. Austria is commended for identifying key areas on which to focus its efforts to make its policies more development friendly.

While Austria has made progress since the last peer review, it could make further efforts to ensure development concerns are better understood and discussed across government. For example, the OECD reports that Austria's performance against key international standards for countering illicit financial flows from developing countries remains modest and that more could be done to combat economic and financial crimes (OECD, 2013). Similarly, according to the 2014 Sustainable Governance Indicators report, challenges remain for Austria in reducing its greenhouse gas emissions and improving financial transparency (Bertelsmann Foundation, 2014).[2] Translating its political commitment to policy coherence for development into practice and actual policy changes will require Austria to set out clearly a path for creating synergies between development and other domestic and foreign policy objectives in a win-win scenario, so that all policies pull together to support development goals.

Moreover, to rally political support to address difficult coherence issues, including in its parliament, Austria could build on the success of past initiatives such as the Development Jour Fixe, which showed the effectiveness of bringing Austrian stakeholders together to raise public awareness of development-related issues. The annual 3C Retreat at the Schlaining Peace Castle is another good example of bringing together relevant actors from government and civil society organisations (CSOs) to foster joint learning and co-operation in the security sector. Putting in place a systematic process for engaging with the wider public to educate and raise awareness of government commitments that support policy coherence for development could contribute to fostering lasting policy change.

Box 1.1 Austria's efforts towards policy coherence for development in security and development

Austria regards the achievement of security and peace as one of the most pressing issues of international development co-operation. It recognises that development and security are interdependent, and that engagement in fragile states or situations requires a holistic approach to development. In 2010 relevant actors from across the Austrian administration and NGO community agreed on a framework, the Vienna 3C Appeal, which sets out the principles for "co-ordinated, complementary and coherent" (3C) measures in fragile situations. Building on these principles, Austria has developed a strategic guideline which incorporates policy coherence for development into its policy framework for security and development, promoting a whole-of-country approach (involving civil society) to engagement in fragile states. The guideline was a joint effort of the MFA, the Federal Ministry of Defence and Sports, the Austrian Development Agency (ADA) and the Austrian Institute for International Affairs. Policy co-ordination and dialogue are conducted through various formal and informal channels, including the Advisory Board of the Foreign Affairs Minister. In addition, Austrian actors involved in security and development are invited to participate in an annual workshop, the 3C Retreat, where projects and strategies on evolving issues are discussed jointly.

Source: MFA (2011).

Except in the areas of environment and security, Austria uses informal channels to co-ordinate policies across government

Policy co-ordination appears to be working successfully in the areas of environment and security; there is regular dialogue[3] between relevant ministries to monitor implementation of the cross-ministerial strategic guidelines and to ensure coherent positions whenever these are required. However, in most other areas informal channels are frequently used to communicate and co-ordinate across federal ministries and with other stakeholders. Efforts appear to be largely ad hoc, focusing on special issues as they arise and when there is a need for a cross-government approach to achieve a particular goal. Similarly, at the political level there is no evidence to suggest that regular discussions on policy coherence for development are held within the parliament or the Council of Ministers.

While the Federal Act on Development Co-operation provides the legal basis for the Federal Ministry for Europe, Integration and Foreign Affairs (MFA) to act as the main conduit for ensuring policy coherence for development, the role of the MFA appears to be largely limited to co-ordinating official development assistance (ODA) policies. Thus criteria for managing trade-offs between competing priorities, and resolving issues of incoherence, are not clear. The MFA acknowledges the need to build greater awareness of policy coherence for development across government – often understood by other ministries as co-ordinating development policy and interventions – and the need for a political directive defining a broader role of government. In this regard, the Advisory Board of the Foreign Affairs Minister might be better used for discussing coherence issues (Chapter 4).

Adequate systems are lacking for analysing potential areas of policy conflicts and for policy arbitration

Austria recognises the importance of development education in raising public awareness and building support for development (Chapter 6). Nevertheless, little appears to have been done to improve awareness of the need to take account of the impact of Austria's non-ODA policies (e.g. trade, agriculture, illicit flows) on the development prospects of developing countries).

Austria contributes to the EU's biennial report on policy coherence for development and to the OECD's *Better Policies for Development Report*. However, it does not report to its parliament or the wider public on progress in making policies development friendly. Like many DAC members, Austria lacks the institutional mechanisms and the capacity to systematically measure, monitor, analyse and report the impact of its domestic and foreign policies on development; this makes it difficult for Austria to determine what changes to these policies might make them more coherent with development objectives.

Debates on policy coherence (e.g. with respect to Austria's bilateral investment protection treaties and their impact on developing countries) are frequently triggered by think tanks and NGOs. The MFA could reinforce its capacity by drawing more on these actors' knowledge and experience to gather sound evidence to underpin inter-ministerial discussions on coherence issues.

Engaging in partner countries: a co-ordinated government approach at partner country level

Indicator: Strategic framework, institutional structures and mechanisms facilitate coherent action

Austria's strategies at partner country level do not yet cover all of its activities or interventions. For example, in Moldova there is no formalised system for co-ordinating the activities of the different Austrian stakeholders involved. Whole-of-government country strategies and objectives would facilitate a more co-ordinated approach at the operational level in partner countries.

A more co-ordinated approach at country level requires whole-of-government strategies

While, in principle, the Three-Year Programme on Austrian Development Policy 2013-2015 serves as the main co-ordination rallying point for all Austrian development activities, Austria's strategies at partner country level do not yet cover all official Austrian actors (Chapter 2). As the review team observed in Moldova, a co-ordinated approach at partner country level is difficult without a whole-of-government approach, lowering the possibility of achieving synergies.

In Moldova there is no formalised system for co-ordinating the activities of the different Austrian stakeholders involved in the field. Co-ordination efforts appear largely informal and ad hoc. The Austrian Development Cooperation (ADC) office's work plan for Moldova only covers activities that it directly administers. While the ADC office solicits the expertise of line ministry attachés and consultants to the extent possible, and in response to specific needs, this does not replace a systematised whole-of-government approach to Austria's development co-operation.

Moreover, making Austria's overall programme more coherent, effective and efficient at country level requires strengthening the ADC office's role and responsibilities (Chapter 4). The fact that the single brand "Austrian Development Cooperation" is not universally adopted by all Austrian ministries is symptomatic of this challenge.[4] The planned regional strategy for the Danube Region/Western Balkans provides an opportunity to set out clearly a holistic approach for internal co-ordination among participating ministries based on common, or at least complementary, priorities for this region.

Financing for development

Indicator: The member engages in development finance in addition to ODA

Private flows to developing countries consistently remain the greatest source of financing from Austria. ODA is also promoted as a catalyst for increasing private flows to support development efforts in partner countries. However, Austria's approach could focus more on ensuring synergies and better outcomes in terms of poverty reduction, in addition to the focus on individual business-to-business relationships. Austria reports non-ODA flows to developing countries, mainly in the form of non-concessional development finance, officially supported export credits, foreign direct investment (FDI) and private charitable grants.

Austria promotes ODA as a catalyst for increasing private flows, but should not lose sight of development objectives

Austria promotes ODA as a catalyst for private investment in support of development efforts in partner countries. Using aid in this way is increasingly important for Austria due to the strong focus on private sector development outlined in the Three-Year Programme and guided by the 2010 Private Sector and Development guidelines. Dialogue between the public and private sectors is promoted through the CorporAID Platform, which helps raise public awareness of private sector engagement in development co-operation.[5] However, there does not appear to be a mechanism for co-ordinating these public and private sector actors in order to maximise private investment for sustainable development.

Since the last peer review (OECD, 2009), Austria has raised substantial amounts of non-ODA funds in addition to its traditional ODA engagement through its small but fast-growing development finance institution, the Austrian Development Bank.[6] Given its increased emphasis on deepening private sector engagement in development co-operation, Austria's approach could focus more on ensuring synergies and better outcomes in terms of poverty reduction, in addition to the focus on individual business-to-business relationships. Developing a broad-based strategy for the role of the private sector in development, with a clear focus on poverty reduction and sustainable development, would be useful in this context, building on ADC's new manual concerning Making Markets Work for the Poor (M4P). The Austrian Development Agency (ADA) and the Development Bank should also continue to co-ordinate and look for synergies to achieve greater development impact.

Austria is increasing its efforts to leverage private flows for development, but it needs to monitor their development impact

Austria has aid-funded support programmes for increasing private contributions in support of development efforts in partner countries. Austrian companies looking for long term engagement in developing countries can directly benefit from an ADA-financed subsidy scheme called the Business Partnership Programme (up to 50% of the total costs, capped at EUR 200 000) on condition that their projects are commercially viable and provide added development benefits. The planned evaluation of the programme will present an opportunity to ensure its approach creates synergies and delivers on inclusive poverty reduction results.

Austria's export credit agency, Oesterreichische Kontrollbank AG, also offers soft loans (tied aid credits) to developing countries including the least developed countries (LDCs).[7] While the Federal Ministry of Finance (MoF) has political responsibility for the soft loan programme,[8] the MFA and other key stakeholders are involved in the approval of projects.[9] Inclusion of the MFA assures that aspects related to sustainability and of developmental relevance are incorporated in the assessment of all soft loan projects. However, there are no formal links between soft loan and ADC programmes even in priority countries. Moreover, the export credit agency does not appear to either monitor or evaluate the development results of its soft loans (Fritz et al., 2014).

At the multilateral level, Austria participates in a number of innovative "blending facilities" (e.g. the EU-Africa Infrastructure Trust Fund and the Western Balkans Investment Framework) and is a member of the EU Platform for Blending in External Cooperation. It also supports the Private Infrastructure Development Group, a multi-donor programme to leverage private finance for infrastructure development in developing countries. Austria has contributed over USD 20 million to this programme since it became a member in 2006.

Austria's private flows to developing countries far exceed its official flows

Austria reports non-ODA flows to the OECD (Annex Table B.1). Private flows to developing countries are consistently the greatest source of financing from Austria. In 2012 Austria's net private flows at market terms to developing countries reached USD 3.4 billion, most of which was FDI outflows to middle-income countries in Europe. In the same year, export credit from Austria's export credit agency amounted to USD 398 million in gross terms, extended either in the form of associated financing (other official flows totalled USD 148 million in 2012) or export credit guarantees to European countries (USD 251 million). In 2012 the export credit agency's subsidiary, the Austrian Development Bank, also disbursed around USD 106 million in net terms, half of which was in Sub-Saharan Africa. Net outflows from Austrian private philanthropic organisations averaged USD 178 million between 2008 and 2012 (USD 263 million in 2012).

Notes

1. Austria was ranked tenth overall in the 2013 Commitment to Development Index (CGD, 2013). Its admission of a large number of legal immigrants from developing countries, relatively low agricultural tariffs, and participation in international security treaties were acknowledged.

2. The Bertelsmann Foundation's Sustainable Governance Indicators is a cross-national comparative survey designed to identify and foster successes in effective policy making (www.sgi-network.org). Based on a broad range of quantitative and qualitative data, these indicators measure how 41 OECD and EU governments target sustainable development. They provide a detailed picture of each country's strengths and weaknesses in terms of sustainable governance. The survey is built on three pillars: i) policy performance; ii) democracy; and iii) governance. Four of its qualitative indicators are directly linked to, or relevant to, policy coherence for development. These are: i) tackling global social inequalities; ii) fostering stable international financial markets; iii) promoting global environmental protection regimes; and iv) creating international co-ordination capacities to foster global public goods (Bertelsmann Foundation, 2014; OECD, 2014).

3. According to the MFA, the inter-ministerial group on Environment and Development meets four times a year and the group on Security and Development meets at least once a month to discuss pending issues, such as the EU's comprehensive approach to external conflicts and crises.

4. In Moldova both the Austrian Federal Ministry for Education and Women's Affairs and the Federal Ministry of Labour, Social Affairs and Consumer Protection were using their respective ministry logos in place of the ADC brand for their projects.

5. Federal Ministry of Science, Research and Economy, "CorporAID platform for business development and global responsibility", www.en.bmwfw.gv.at/ExternalTrade/InternationalisationInitiative/Seiten/CorporAID.aspx.

6. Compared to commercial banks, the Austrian Development Bank is in a position to assume higher risks on individual financing transactions given its special development mandate (it obtains a guarantee from the Federal Ministry of Finance to cover commercial and political risks). The Bank offers three instruments to finance private sector projects in developing countries: non-concessional loans, equity participation (since 2012), and ODA-eligible grants for project-supporting measures (identifying, preparing, inspecting, monitoring and implementing projects) called Advisory Programmes.

7. Currently 24 countries (including 9 LDCs: Angola, Ethiopia, Lesotho, Mozambique, Myanmar, Senegal, Tanzania, Uganda and Zambia) are eligible for soft loan financing from the export credit agency. In addition, Indonesia, the Philippines and Sri Lanka benefit from special measures for soft loan financing which focus on projects that have a short implementation period with transaction limits of EUR 5 to 8 million. The loans offered are in line with the OECD Arrangement on Officially Supported Export Credits (i.e. a concessionality level of at least 35%). For LDCs, soft loans must have a grant element of at least 50%. The terms and conditions currently offered under this soft loan scheme are available in English at www.oekb.at.

8. Given its particular development policy motivation, the MoF offers a reduction of the guarantee charges, which lowers total costs for the recipient country. The MoF also provides financial grants for the identification/preparation of soft loan projects in

eligible soft loan countries. Financial support by the MoF for the soft loan scheme constitutes a part of Austrian ODA.

9. The members of the export financing committee include the MoF (Chair), the MFA, the Austrian Chamber of Commerce, the Austrian Chamber of Labour and the Federal inistry of Economic Affairs, with Austria's export credit agency and the National Bank of Austria as non-voting members. The export guarantee committee comprises the members of the export financing committee and representatives of the Federal Chancellery, the Federal Ministry of Agriculture and Environmental Affairs, the Chamber of Agriculture, the Federation of Trade Unions, and the National Bank.

Bibliography

Government sources

GoA (Federal Government of Austria) (2013), *Work Programme of the Austrian Federal Government 2013-2018: Austria. A Story of Success*, Austrian Federal Chancellery, Vienna, www.bka.gv.at/DocView.axd?CobId=53588.

GoA et al. (2010), *Vienna 3C Appeal: Coordinated, Complementary and Coherent Measures in Fragile Situations. Principles and Aims of Interaction between Government and Non-governmental Actors. Recommendations*, Vienna, www.entwicklung.at/uploads/media/Vienna_3C_Appeal.pdf.

MFA (Federal Ministry for Europe, Integration and Foreign Affairs) (2014), *OECD DAC Peer Review of Austria: Memorandum*, April 2014, MFA, Vienna.

MFA (2012), *Three Year Programme on Austrian Development Policy 2013-2015*, MFA, Vienna, www.entwicklung.at/uploads/media/ThreeYearProgramme_13-15_02.pdf.

MFA (2011), *Security and Development in Austrian Development Policy: Strategic Guideline*, MFA, Vienna, www.entwicklung.at/uploads/media/StratGuide_Security_and_Development.pdf.

Other sources

Bertelsmann Foundation (2014), *Sustainable Governance Indicators: 2014 Austria Report*, Bertelsmann Stiftung, Gütersloh, Germany, www.sgi-network.org/docs/2014/country/SGI2014_Austria.pdf.

CGD (Center for Global Development) (2013), *Austria, Commitment to Development Index 2013*, CGD, Washington, D.C., www.cgdev.org/sites/default/files/archive/doc/CDI_2013/Country_13_Austria_EN.pdf.

EU (European Union) (2013a), *Working Document: EU Report on Policy Coherence for Development*, SWD(2013)456 final, 31 October 2013, EU, Brussels, http://register.consilium.europa.eu/doc/srv?l=EN&f=ST%2015646%202013%20INIT.

EU (2013b), "Council Conclusions on Policy Coherence for Development", 12 December 2013, EU, Brussels, www.consilium.europa.eu/uedocs/cms_data/docs/pressdata/EN/foraff/140063.pdf.

EU (2009), "Council Conclusions on Policy Coherence for Development", 17 November 2009, EU, Brussels, www.consilium.europa.eu/uedocs/cms_Data/docs/pressdata/en/gena/111278.pdf.

Fritz, L. et al. (2014), *Export Promotion or Development Policy? A Comparative Analysis of Soft Loan Policies in Austria, Denmark, Germany and the Netherlands*, Austrian Foundation for Development Research (ÖFSE), Südwind Publishing, Vienna.

OECD (2014), *Better Policies for Development 2014: Policy Coherence and Illicit Financial Flows*, OECD Publishing, Paris, http://dx.doi.org/10.1787/9789264210325-en.

OECD (2013), *Measuring OECD Reponses to Illicit Financial Flows from Developing Countries*, OECD Publishing, Paris, http://dx.doi.org/10.1787/9789264203501-en.

OECD (2009), *Austria: Development Assistance Committee (DAC) Peer Review*, OECD Publishing, Paris, http://dx.doi.org/10.1787/1996580x.

OECD (2008), "Ministerial Declaration on Policy Coherence for Development", OECD, Paris, http://acts.oecd.org/Instruments/ShowInstrumentView.aspx?InstrumentID=138&InstrumentPID=134&Lang=en&Book=False.

Chapter 2: Austria's vision and policies for development co-operation

Policies, strategies and commitments

Indicator: A clear policy vision and solid strategies guide the programme

Austria's 2003 Federal Act on Development Co-operation and the Three-Year Programme 2013-2015 provide the legal and strategic focus for Austria's ODA programme, with poverty reduction at the centre. The Three-Year Programme is considered the medium-term policy for Austria's development co-operation. However, it does not cover the entire Austrian system. Bringing all aid-spending ministries in line with the three-year programmes, and making them accountable for meeting the objectives of the programmes, would contribute to improving the coherence and effectiveness of Austria's development co-operation. Austria has formulated policies and strategies for most of its priority sectors and themes. When updating these documents, it should take its comparative advantage into account, as well as where Austria's development co-operation is needed most.

The mission statement on development co-operation has broad ownership; the three-year programmes could be more inclusive

The overall framework for Austrian Development Cooperation (ADC) is set out in the Federal Ministries Act (1986) and the 2002 Federal Act on Development Co-operation (amended in 2003). Legislation is complemented by three-year programmes, elaborated by the Federal Ministry for Europe, Integration and Foreign Affairs (MFA), and approved by the Cabinet. In 2012 a "mission statement" was included as the preface to the Three-Year Programme on Austrian Development Policy 2013-2015. The mission statement identified the overall purpose of Austria's development co-operation as well as its main priorities. It was drafted in consultation with a number of stakeholders and has wide ownership.

The Three-Year Programme 2013-2015 (MFA, 2012a) is considered the medium-term policy for Austria's development co-operation. It is more strategic and result-oriented than previous rolling triennial programmes, and a number of federal ministries contributed to it at some stage. However, it is not a binding "white paper" covering the entire Austrian system, as recommended by the DAC in the 2009 peer review (OECD, 2009). More inclusive three-year programmes, bringing all aid-spending ministries in line with these programmes, and making them accountable for meeting the objectives of the programmes, would contribute to improving the coherence and effectiveness of ADC. A financing framework allowing for multi-annual budgetary planning would also make the three-year programmes more binding and transparent. Several representatives from Austrian civil society, the private sector and parliament reported that they were not sufficiently involved in the process leading to the elaboration of the Three-Year Programme 2013-2015. In preparing future programmes the government is encouraged to engage in a more structured dialogue with these actors.

Poverty reduction features prominently in policy documents

Poverty reduction is at the centre of the Federal Act on Development Co-operation (GoA, 2003). The Federal Act relates poverty reduction to the promotion of democracy, the rule of law, human rights and good governance, as well as the protection of the environment and natural resources. The Three-Year Programme 2013-2015 makes explicit reference to the most vulnerable groups and to pro-poor economic growth. It also confirms Austria's commitment to the 0.7% ODA/gross national income (GNI) target, the Millennium Development Goals (MDGs), and the Busan Partnership for Effective Development Co-operation. The government's 2013 2018 Work Programme declares Austria's obligation vis-à-vis people in the poorest and most disadvantaged regions and countries to be a central responsibility of Austrian foreign policy (GoA, 2013).

Austria covers a wide range of sectors relative to its limited ODA resources

The sectoral scope of ADC is broad given Austria's limited bilateral resources. It covers three clusters (water supply, energy, climate protection, agriculture and forestry; the private sector and development; and human security, human rights and rule of law), as well as three cross-cutting themes (gender equality; the environment and climate change; and education and capacity development). Austria is committed to focusing on two to three sectors in each priority country, and has formulated policies and strategies for most of its priority sectors and themes.[1] A number of these documents need to better reflect the changing global context and Austria's funding realities, and to be supported by appropriate operational guidance. When updating its policy documents, Austria should take its comparative advantage into account, as well as where ADC is needed most. This would help managers to prioritise their interventions.

Decision-making

Indicator: The rationale for allocating aid and other resources is clear and evidence-based

Austria is committed to implementing the EU development agenda, and seeks to influence that agenda. It has a strategic approach with respect to international financial institutions. However, Austria does not have a clear rationale for allocating resources among recipient countries, regions and channels. Allocation criteria are necessary to safeguard predictability for partners and Austrian actors alike. Well-defined objectives vis-à-vis Austria's key United Nations partners are also needed.

Austria's approach for allocating aid resources by country and region is vague

Austria's Three-Year Programme 2013-2015 states that the least developed countries (LDCs), European neighbours and fragile states are "at the heart of Austria's approach to allocating resources." However, the programme does not provide a sufficient rationale or basis for allocating these resources among recipient countries, channels and instruments. The lack of criteria and a clear narrative for Austria's engagement also apply to Austria's regional programmes, particularly in the Caribbean, Himalayas-Hindu Kush, West Africa and Southern Africa.[2] Allocation criteria are necessary to safeguard predictability for partners and Austrian actors alike.

Austria uses country data and indicators to the extent possible

The Three-Year Programme 2013-2015 states that Austria is motivated by "direct control, the use of Austrian know-how, high visibility both abroad and at home, complementarity with the United Nations (UN) and the international financial institutions (IFIs), and giving Austria a voice in the European Union (EU)" (MFA, 2012a). While these criteria apply across Austria's development co-operation, in reality the top recipients of Austrian bilateral ODA are primarily determined by debt relief operations, in-donor refugee costs and imputed student costs (Chapter 3).

In partner countries Austria states that it "strives to align with people's needs, strengthen bilateral relations with recipient countries, and harness synergies with foreign policy, and debt relief." In Moldova, Austria's action is consistent with the EU's European Neighbourhood Policy and its country strategy is effectively aligned with the priorities of the Moldovan government. The field office endeavours to target Austria's multi-bi contributions with a view to developing synergies with its bilateral activities, and uses national data and indicators to the extent possible when elaborating its country strategies. This is considered good practice. Austria reports that due to time, resource and capacity constraints, it cannot provide support to local partners in data collection and analysis in all its interventions.

The approach to the IFIs shows a clear profile; the approach to UN organisations could be more strategic

Working with and through the EU, and supporting the IFIs, constitute the main rationale for Austria's multilateral policy (MFA, 2012a). The MFA is committed to implementing the EU development agenda and seeks to influence that agenda. It has set up a unit specifically dealing with EU instruments and aims, among other things, at better aligning EU aid to Austria's geographic (neighbouring countries) focus.[3]

The Federal Ministry of Finance (MoF) has developed strategic guidelines for the IFIs and monitors their performance closely. Multi-bi contributions are targeted "with a view to reaping synergies with other ADC actors and interventions, and enhancing the visibility and effectiveness of Austrian support" (MFA, 2014). The MoF endeavours to develop synergies in accordance with the orientations of the Three-Year Programme and to concentrate its contributions to the IFIs on priority themes (with the exception of urban development, which is not a priority of the triennial programme).

The MFA makes decisions concerning UN funds and programmes based on three criteria: i) an objective evaluation of the respective entity; ii) the priorities defined in the three-year programmes; and iii) Austria's interests as the host country of some organisations. Austria is a member of the Multilateral Organisation Performance Assessment Network (MOPAN). However, the means by which it uses the MOPAN as a basis for making strategic decisions (the first criteria) is unclear. Its funding is spread over six main organisations (Chapter 3). These contributions have become unpredictable, mostly as a result of decreases in Austrian ODA. Austria should set out well-defined objectives vis-à-vis its key UN partners, and be clearer about its intentions to grant voluntary contributions over time to increase the predictability of its aid to them.

Policy focus

Indicator: Fighting poverty, especially in LDCs and fragile states, is prioritised

Austria's poverty strategy covers a broad spectrum. When reflecting on its approach to poverty reduction, Austria needs to be realistic about what it can achieve and focus on areas where it can add value. Linking the priorities for reducing poverty to result-oriented methodologies, and tools for reporting and learning would be useful. Guidance on working in fragile contexts has increased dialogue on these issues; next steps include focusing Austria's priorities in each fragile state and designing programmes with a fragility lens. Given its limited ODA resources, Austria is encouraged to clarify its priorities for mainstreaming cross-cutting issues throughout its development co-operation and ensure that it has the tools and resources to follow-through on these priorities.

The poverty strategy covers a broad spectrum; focusing on areas where Austria can add value would be useful

Austria's 2009 poverty strategy covers a broad spectrum, from basic livelihoods, to social and economic services, political and democratic framework conditions, and to social protection and risk minimisation. The strategy states that Austria relies on national poverty reduction strategies and sector strategies for its interventions and that it monitors progress and identifies adverse developmental effects using comprehensive poverty assessments based on indicators and representative data (MFA, 2009a). In doing so, Austria relies on existing poverty assessments conducted by the partner country or other donors. One good example of collaboration took place in Albania, where ADC and the Swiss Agency for Development and Cooperation (SDC) jointly financed a programme on regional development using *ex ante* poverty impact assessments.

When reflecting on its approach to poverty reduction, Austria should set clear objectives focusing on areas where it can add value, and linking its priorities for reducing poverty to result-oriented methodologies and tools for reporting and learning. The strategy and the manual on poverty reduction, which the Austrian Development Agency is currently elaborating, should be closely related.

No formal links between humanitarian and development programming

Human security, human rights and the rule of law are thematic priorities of Austria's 2013-2015 aid programme. Austria was working in five fragile contexts at the time of this peer review.[4] It reports that all its programmes in fragile states take into account peacebuilding and statebuilding goals (MFA, 2014); how this is done in practice is not entirely clear (Chapter 5). Although Austria's funding to NGOs can be multi-annual and thus allow them to incorporate recovery elements as the context evolves, there are no formal links between humanitarian and development programmes, even in priority countries (Chapter 7).

Guidance for fragile contexts has increased dialogue on these issues; next steps include refining priorities and programming with a fragility lens

The security and development guideline (MFA, 2011) seeks to achieve a comprehensive, whole-of-government approach to human security, recognising the centrality of the Fragile States Principles. It outlines a broad range of priorities for Austrian programmes,[5] encouraging Austrian actors to engage in many different areas of conflict prevention, crisis management, and peacebuilding and statebuilding. The peer review team heard that the guideline and a focus paper on fragility encouraged dialogue on fragility issues across government through a new permanent working group, which includes members from the ADA, the MFA, the Ministry of Defence and Sports, NGOs and Austrian think tanks.

The next challenge will be to make sure programmes in fragile contexts are designed with this guideline in mind. Narrowing the scope of Austria's priorities, by focusing on areas where it can clearly add value, could be a useful next step. The planned review of the security and development guideline could provide a useful opportunity for Austria to reinforce its political commitments to fragility, and to develop guidance on how to design programmes with a fragility lens.

Policy guidance for mainstreaming cross-cutting issues is in place; programming tools and tailored training are needed at field level

Austria's environment-related development co-operation is guided by the Strategic Guidelines on Environment and Development in Austrian Development Policy (MFA, 2009b) and by its focus papers. Its policy on gender equality and empowerment of women (MFA, 2006) is complemented by guidance on gender sensitive budgeting and gender evaluations, as well as focus papers on gender-related issues. Gender-related issues are present in the triennial programmes and most other policy documents of ADC, albeit with varying degrees of emphasis and scope. For example, the guidelines on environment and development explicitly underline women's empowerment, gender equality and gender mainstreaming. The guidelines on security and development refer to the protection needs of women and children and discuss contributions to the implementation of UN Security Council resolution 1325 on women and peace and security.

A recent independent evaluation of the gender equality policy showed mixed results and recommended updating this policy (ADA, 2012). The recommendations, such as decentralising gender competence to the field level, are followed up by a management response. Austria reports that this will be accompanied by a series of trainings and the development of a practical toolkit to support the systematic integration of a gender perspective into the policy dialogue and main sectors, such as energy and water. While the OECD has praised Austria for its comprehensive framework for sustainable development, it has noted that climate change adaptation has been neglected compared to mitigation, and has recommended improving the strategic focus and linkages with other environmental issues (OECD, 2013a).

As is the case for many other DAC members, mainstreaming cross-cutting issues continues to be work-in-progress for Austria. Austria's intention to allocate 10% of bilateral ODA to biodiversity activities, and its ambitious target of 75% gender-relevant projects in the ADA's business plan, have not been realised to date.[6] As observed in Moldova, in dealing with gender equality and the environment, ADC combines specific targeted activities with some mainstreaming. However, the programme did not benefit from specific gender expertise and field staff did not receive the tailored gender training they needed.[7] Given its limited ODA resources, Austria is encouraged to clarify its priorities for mainstreaming cross-cutting issues throughout its development co-operation. It should then ensure that it has the tools and resources to follow-through on these priorities.

Notes

1. Austria has policy and strategic documents on poverty reduction (2009); budget support (2009); gender equality and the empowerment of women (2006); good governance (2006); human rights (2006); energy for sustainable development (2006); peacebuilding and conflict prevention (2006); higher education and scientific co-operation (2009); development communication and education (2010); environment and development (2009); the private sector and development (2010); and security and development (2011). The ADA has also produced "focus papers" on: agriculture and food security; corruption; children; democratic ownership; fragility; the green economy; climate change; women, gender and armed conflicts; disabled people; health; water and sanitation; humanitarian assistance and decentralised co-operation.

2. Austria's Memorandum states that regional programmes are "concentrating on problems identified by several countries in a given region as common challenge that cannot be tackled properly or successfully on an individual basis" (MFA, 2014).

3. For example, the Foreign and European Policy Report 2012 (MFA, 2012b) links Austria's engagement in the Danube and Western Balkans to the EU Strategy for the Danube Region, which Austria states it initiated.

4. The five fragile contexts are Burkina Faso, Ethiopia, Kosovo, the West Bank and Gaza Strip, and Uganda (according to the OECD/DAC 2014 list of fragile states).

5. The Guideline covers conflict prevention, crisis management, and peacebuilding and state-building. It recognises the importance of gender, the protection of civilians and socio-economic perspectives in these broad programmes. A wide range of activities are listed as priorities for each of the themes.

6. This could partly be due to the particular nature of Austrian bilateral ODA, i.e. very limited country programmable aid (Chapter 3).

7. All heads of ADA field offices (ADC co-ordination offices) are briefed on ADC's policies on the environment, and on gender equality and women's empowerment, before being deployed.

Bibliography

Government sources

ADA (Austrian Development Agency) (2013), *Evaluation: Private Sector Development of the Austrian Development Cooperation. Final Report*, ADA, Vienna, www.oecd.org/derec/austria/Evaluation_private_sector_final_report_01.pdf.

ADA (2012), *Evaluation of the Austrian Development Cooperation (ADC) Gender Policy between 2004-2011. Final Report*, ADA, Vienna, www.oecd.org/derec/austria/Final%20Evaluation%20Report%20GENDER.pdf.

GoA (Federal Government of Austria) (2013), *Work Programme of the Austrian Federal Government 2013-2018: Austria. A Story of Success*, Austrian Federal Chancellery, Vienna, www.bka.gv.at/DocView.axd?CobId=53588.

GoA (2003), "Federal Act on Development Cooperation (2002), Including its Amendment (2003)", GoA, Vienna, www.entwicklung.at/uploads/media/development_cooperation_law_01.pdf.

MFA (Federal Ministry for Europe, Integration and Foreign Affairs) (2014), *OECD DAC Peer Review of Austria: Memorandum*, April 2014, MFA, Vienna.

MFA (2012a), *Three Year Programme on Austrian Development Policy 2013-2015*, MFA, Vienna, www.entwicklung.at/uploads/media/ThreeYearProgramme_13-15.pdf.

MFA (2012b), *Foreign and European Policy Report 2012 – Report by the Federal Minister for European and International Affairs*, MFA, Vienna, www.bmeia.gv.at/en/the-ministry/foreign-and-european-policy-report/.

MFA (2011), *Security and Development in Austrian Development Policy. Strategic Guideline*, MFA, Vienna, www.entwicklung.at/uploads/media/StratGuide_Security_and_Development.pdf.

MFA (2010), *Three-Year Programme on Austrian Development Policy 2010-2012. Revised Version 2010*, MFA, Vienna, www.entwicklung.at/uploads/media/Three-YearProgramme10-12_03.pdf.

MFA (2009a), *Poverty Reduction: Policy Document*, MFA, Vienna, www.entwicklung.at/uploads/media/PD_Poverty_reduction_Dec2009_01.pdf.

MFA (2009b), *Strategic Guideline on Environment and Development in Austrian Development Policy*, MFA, Vienna, www.entwicklung.at/uploads/media/Web_ADC_Leitfaden_Umwelt_Entwicklung_engl_01.pdf.

MFA (2006), *Gender Equality and Empowerment of Women: Policy Document*, MFA, Vienna, www.entwicklung.at/uploads/media/PD_Gender_Equality_19032010_Web.pdf.

Other sources

EU (European Union) (2011), *Increasing the Impact of EU Development Policy: An Agenda for Change*, COM (2011) 637 final, European Commission, Brussels, http://ec.europa.eu/europeaid/infopoint/publications/europeaid/257a_en.htm.

OECD (2013a), *Environmental Performance Reviews: Austria*, OECD Publishing, Paris, http://dx.doi.org/10.1787/9789264202924-en.

OECD (2013b), *Multilateral Aid Report – The Development Assistance Committee: Enabling Effective Development*, OECD Publishing, Paris, www.oecd.org/dac/aid-architecture/DCD_DAC(2012)33_FINAL.pdf.

OECD (2009), *Austria: Development Assistance Committee (DAC) Peer Review,* OECD Publishing, Paris, http://dx.doi.org/10.1787/1996580x.

Chapter 3: Allocating Austria's official development assistance

Overall ODA volume

Indicator: The member makes every effort to meet ODA domestic and international targets

Austria's ODA volume declined substantially in 2009, but it has stayed stable since. However, cuts in the ODA budget are foreseen in 2015 and beyond, which risks hampering Austria's ability to realise the ambitions outlined in its policy documents. The government's intention to develop a legally binding roadmap to achieve the 0.7% UN target for ODA/GNI is positive step forward. Debt relief should be included in Austria's ODA projections only after this is agreed by the Paris Club. Austria is also encouraged to resume the long-standing high quality reporting of its statistics to the DAC.

Decreasing levels of ODA prevent Austria from meeting its EU and international aid targets

Austria's aid levels – both in terms of volume and as a share of national income – declined substantially in 2009, mostly as a result of the drop in debt relief operations, which were exceptionally high between 2005 and 2008. However, Austria has managed to keep its ODA volume stable since then. Its net ODA in 2013 amounted to USD 1.2 billion (preliminary data), an increase of 0.7% in real terms from 2012, and the equivalent of 0.28% of gross national income (GNI). While planned ODA budget cuts for 2013 and 2014, as part of cross-governmental budget cuts to reduce budget deficits,[1] were put on hold, further cuts are foreseen in 2015 and beyond. This may prevent Austria from realising the ambitions outlined in the Three-Year Programme 2013-2015.

Austria fell short of meeting its interim target of 0.51% in 2010 (its ODA to GNI ratio for that year was 0.32%) and it will not reach the 2015 ODA target of 0.7%. Despite Austria's continued political commitment to providing 0.7% of GNI as ODA, it has not defined a path for achieving that target. Therefore, the government's intention to develop a legally binding "phased plan to increase [ODA] funds ... until the 0.7 % target is reached" (GoA, 2013) is a positive step forward. Delivering on this commitment would contribute to ensuring the predictability of Austrian aid, as well as Austria's credibility as a donor.

Continued reliance on debt relief undermines the predictability of future aid flows

Austria's bilateral aid is unusual in that it is dominated by debt relief operations. Bilateral ODA allocated to debt relief was high in 2012 (USD 106 million or 19.4% of bilateral aid), more than doubling (a 160% increase) from USD 43 million in 2011. Over the period 2008-12, debt relief accounted for 25% of total bilateral ODA (disbursed) compared to the DAC average of 5.7%.

Contrary to the 2009 peer review recommendation (OECD, 2009), Austria continues to rely on debt relief as a significant component for meeting its ODA commitments. Some large debt cancellations are forecast in its Three-Year Programme: well over EUR 500 million each year in the period 2013-15. This represents more than 60% of Austria's projected bilateral ODA budget. However, inclusion of debt relief before this has been agreed by the Paris Club inflates projections and risks undermining Austria's credibility. There is also a risk in using over-optimistic forecasts based on anticipated debt cancellations, as the failed Paris Club negotiations between Sudan and its creditors in 2012 have demonstrated.

Austria does not engage in bilateral negotiations with its partner countries to discuss development through debt relief or debt-for-development swaps. It considers that the involvement of the Bretton Woods institutions in the Paris Club negotiations ensures developmental benefits in exchange for forgiven debt.

The quality of Austria's statistical reporting has fallen

For many years Austria was among the best performers in terms of the quality and timeliness of its DAC statistical reporting. However, its reporting on ODA appears to have lost its long-standing high quality recently due to resource constraints. Adequate resources are needed to ensure timely and coherent statistical reporting.

In a fiscally constrained environment, managing aid predictability is challenging. Austria publishes forward-looking data through the annual DAC Survey on Aid Allocations and Indicative Forward Spending Plans, and it is rated relatively high in terms of forward-looking information in the Global Partnership monitoring report (OECD/UNDP, 2014). While it conforms to the DAC rules for statistical reporting on ODA, Austria no longer reports activity-level data to the forward spending survey, which limits transparency in the coverage and visibility of its aid activities (Chapter 6). This hampers accountability both domestically and in the international community, putting its credibility at risk.

Figure 3.1 Austria's ODA (USD million)

a) Net ODA volume and percentage of GNI

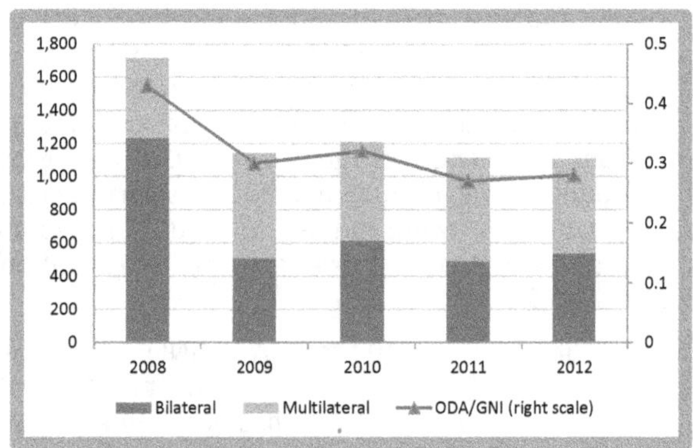

b) Share of debt relief in gross bilateral ODA

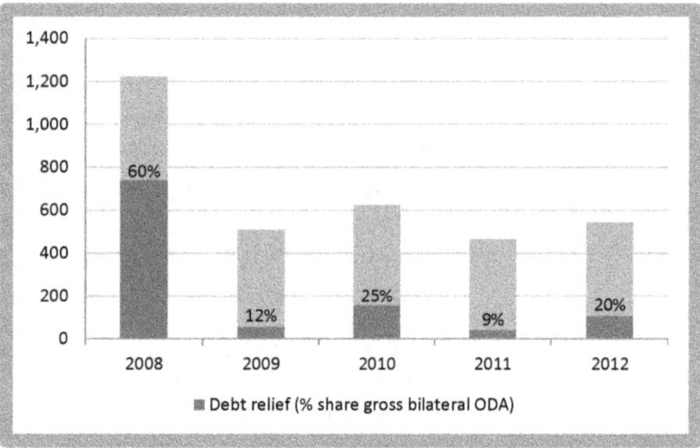

Source: DAC statistics.

Bilateral ODA allocations

Indicator: Aid is allocated according to the statement of intent and international commitments

While Austria's programme is relatively concentrated, its priority partner countries do not figure prominently among the top recipients of Austrian aid. This is mostly due to the small size of country programmable aid. Austria's commitment to maintain a high level of engagement in LDCs is also contradicted by the drop in its bilateral aid to this category of countries since the last peer review. The low level of aid programmed at country level limits what Austria can aspire to as a bilateral donor.

The small size of country programmable aid limits the ambition of Austria's core bilateral programme

Austria's ODA is relatively concentrated. Geographical selectivity is provided through its historical focus on Europe (Chapter 2) and its increasing focus on Sub-Saharan Africa, with USD 131 million and USD 166 million allocated, respectively, in 2012.

While the share of Austria's bilateral aid that is programmed at country level remains small, accounting for 15% (USD 84 million) in 2012, far below the DAC average of 55% (Figure 3.2), its allocations are broadly consistent with the policy priorities defined in ADC's policy papers. Most country programmable aid targets priority countries (Table 3.1) and nearly 45% goes to LDCs, above the DAC average of 37%.

In spite of this, Austria's priority partner countries do not figure prominently among its overall top recipients (Table 3.1)[2] due to the small size of ADC's core programme, represented by its country programmable aid (Figure 3.2). In fact, the proportion of bilateral ODA delivered to Austria's priority countries in 2012 only amounts to 13.9%, with Kosovo receiving the highest share at 2.1% of Austria's bilateral aid.

Similarly Austria's stated poverty focus in its policy documents does not appear to be well reflected in its ODA figures. Its aid to LDCs (gross bilateral allocable by country, excluding debt relief) dropped following the last peer review, from USD 71 million in 2010 to USD 55 million in 2012, representing 12.5% of gross bilateral ODA (compared to the DAC average of 41%). Austria's overall support to LDCs, including through multilateral agencies, accounted for 22% of its total ODA (or 0.06% of GNI) in 2012, well below the DAC average of 32% (Annex Table B.6). Its support to fragile states was USD 196 million (36% of total bilateral ODA) in 2012.

This demonstrates that a low level of country programmable aid limits what Austria can aspire to as a bilateral donor.[3]

Table 3.1 Top recipients of Austrian ODA, 2011-12 average, disbursements (priority partners in bold)

Top ten recipients of gross ODA (2012 USD million)		Top ten recipients of CPA (2012 USD million)	
1. Côte d'Ivoire	50	**1. Uganda**	**10.6**
2. Turkey	36	**2. Mozambique**	**8.3**
3. Bosnia and Herzegovina	27	**3. Ethiopia**	**7.6**
4. China	19	4. Nicaragua	6.3
5. Togo	16	**5. Burkina Faso**	**5.8**
6. Ukraine	12	**6. West Bank and Gaza Strip**	**4.7**
7. Uganda	**12**	**7. Bhutan**	**3.4**
8. Kosovo	**12**	**8. Kosovo**	**3.1**
9. Serbia	11	9. Bosnia and Herzegovina	2.6
10. Ethiopia	**10**	10. Egypt	1.8

Source: DAC statistics. *Note:* CPA: country programmable aid.

Sector allocations reflect Austria's strategic priorities

Austria's overall sectoral allocations appear to reflect its policy priorities, with nearly 60% (USD 339 million) of its total bilateral ODA allocated to social infrastructure and services in 2011-12 (Annex Table B.5). A large part of its support is spent on education,[4] followed by health. Support to economic infrastructure (8%) has also been increasing over the years. While DAC statistics show that Austria supported an average of six sectors in its main partner countries in 2012, giving the impression the aid portfolio is fragmented, this partly reflects Austria's "nexus approach" to implementing its thematic priorities, which often requires a multi-sector approach to be effective (Chapter 2). Sectoral and thematic priorities are reflected in Austria's allocations at partner country level, as the review team observed in Moldova (Annex C).

Austria is a small donor, in terms of volume, in almost all the sectors it supports. In six of its partner countries, however, it ranks among the top donors in a number of sectors: in education in Kosovo, Moldova and Nicaragua; in water supply and sanitation in Uganda; in non-agricultural productive sectors in Nicaragua; and in government and civil society in Bhutan. These sectors are consistent with the priorities in the Three-Year Programme.

Figure 3.2 Composition of Austria's gross bilateral aid programme in 2012

In-donor refugees costs 11%
Other & unallocated 26%
Support to NGOs 0.2%
Admin. costs 6%
Imputed student costs 21%
Country Programmable Aid 15%
Debt relief 18%
Humanitarian & food aid 3%

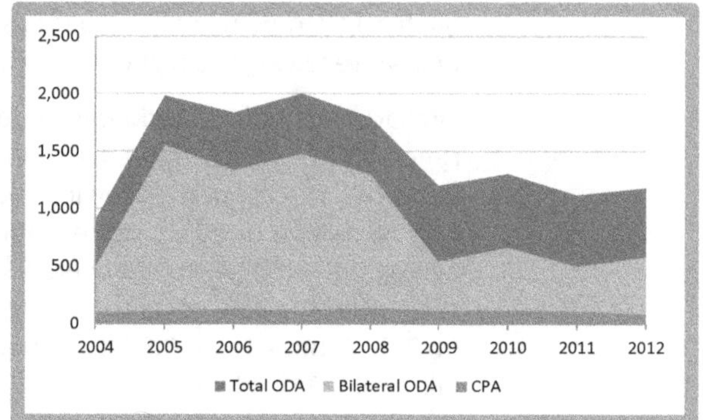

Source: DAC statistics.

Support to gender equality, the environment and NGOs has fallen

Support to gender equality and women's empowerment (Chapter 2) has been declining since the last peer review. The share of gender-focused aid fell from 17% in 2010 to only around 12% in 2012, well below the DAC average of 28% (Figure 3.3). Moreover, only a tiny share of Austria's aid to education and health – the two biggest sectors for ADC – focuses on gender. In terms of geographical distribution, nine of the top ten recipients of Austria's gender-focused aid in 2011-12 were its priority partner countries, with Uganda topping the list (92% of Austria's aid to that country focused on gender equality).

Challenges also remain in mainstreaming the environment, another cross-cutting priority for all Austria's development co-operation (Chapter 2). In 2011-12 only 10% (or USD 57 million) of bilateral ODA had environment as a principal or significant objective, below the DAC average of 27% (Figure 3.3). To improve Austria's share of ODA targeting environmental objectives, further efforts are needed to ensure the goal of mainstreaming environmental objectives is shared by all Austrian actors engaged in development co-operation at all levels.

There is continued commitment to working with NGOs, and funding schemes have been simplified (Chapter 5). However, Austria's stated ambition does not appear to be reflected in its resource allocation. Austrian ODA channelled to and through NGOs halved from USD 90 million in 2009 to USD 45 million in 2012, accounting for only 4% of total net ODA, far below the DAC average of 13% (Annex Table B.1). In the same year, Austria's core support to national NGOs reached only 0.2% of its gross bilateral ODA (Figure 3.2).

Figure 3.3 Cross-cutting issues

Gender equality and women's empowerment
(USD million, % total sector allocable)

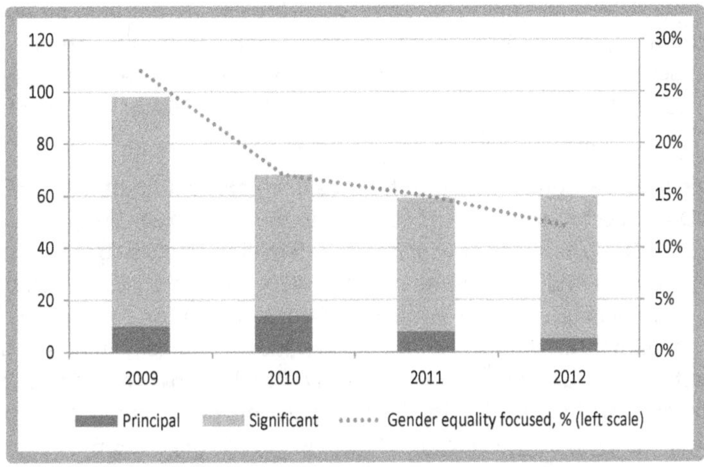

Source: DAC statistics.

Environment-related aid[5]

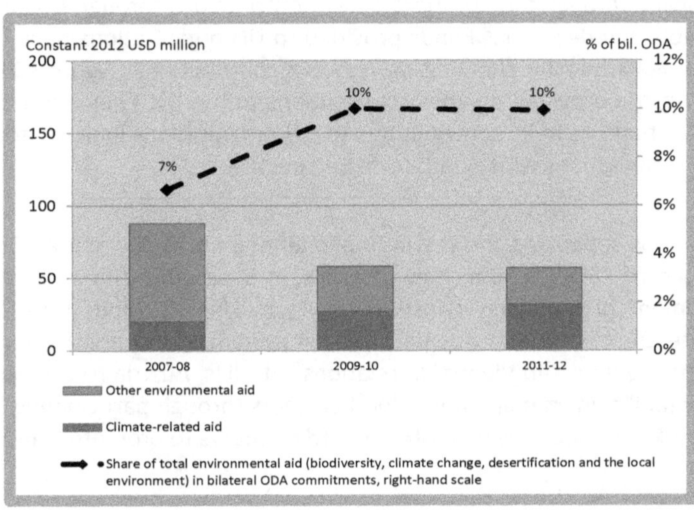

Source: DAC statistics.

Multilateral ODA channels

Indicator: The member uses the multilateral aid channels effectively

Austria's financial contribution to the EU is the largest single item of Austrian ODA, accounting for a quarter of the total ODA budget. The allocation to international financial institutions (IFIs) depends on legally binding agreements with these institutions and accounts for another quarter of Austrian ODA. Austria attaches particular importance to strengthening multilateral organisations that have their headquarters in Vienna. It also actively contributes to the governing boards of IFIs.

Austria's contributions to the EU and IFIs have remained stable, while funds to UN organisations have declined significantly

The general division of Austria's ODA between the multilateral and bilateral channels has remained relatively constant (except for 2008 due to exceptionally high debt relief), with the former accounting for just over 50% of total gross disbursements in recent years (Figure 3.4). The Three-Year Programme provides the basis for determining multilateral aid allocations across multilateral agencies. In 2012 core budget as a share of Austria's total use of the multilateral system (89%) was higher than that of other DAC members (69%) (OECD, forthcoming), and it has committed to increase core funding in its development policy (OECD, 2014). In 2012 Austria allocated 51% of total ODA as core contributions to multilateral organisations, and channelled a further 6% as multi-bi.[6]

Austria's financial contribution to the EU's development co-operation is the largest single item of its ODA, in accordance with its strategy in the Three-Year Programme. In 2012 it contributed a total of USD 277 million (of which USD 275 million as core contributions) to the EU/European Development Fund, accounting for 43% of its total multilateral contributions (OECD, forthcoming). Austria is also a major contributor to key IFIs.[7] The allocation to IFIs, which accounts for another quarter, depends on legally binding agreements with these organisations (Figure 3.5)[8] and is mainly handled by the Federal Ministry of Finance in accordance with its strategy for IFI engagement. Funds going through the EU and IFIs have remained relatively stable since the last peer review (Figure 3.6).

Austria does not make multi-year commitments to the UN organisations. In 2010-13 it made financial contributions to six UN organisations, of which four received core contributions in each of those years (MFA data). However, compared to the proportions of Austrian ODA channelled through the EU and the IFIs, contributions through UN funds and programmes are negligible and declining.[9] Funds provided to UN organisations have decreased dramatically in recent years, mostly affecting MFA's core contributions (Figure 3.7). Due to budget cuts, in 2012 Austria provided no core contributions to the UN Population Fund (UNFPA) or UNAIDS. Such fluctuations in its contributions to UN organisations limit Austria's ability to engage with these organisations with a long-term perspective.

Austria supports joint efforts to increase multilateral effectiveness

Austria has supported the UN in implementing its "Delivering as One" approach. It is also a member of MOPAN, but how it takes into account the results from MOPAN's annual assessment of multilateral institutions in making decisions on aid allocation is not clear (Chapter 2). Austria attaches particular importance to strengthening organisations that have their headquarters in Vienna. In relations with IFIs, Austria (represented by the MoF) ensures accountability in its main multilateral partners through participating in their governing boards and working collectively with other board members to promote transparency.

Figure 3.4 Share of multilateral aid in total gross ODA, constant 2012 USD million

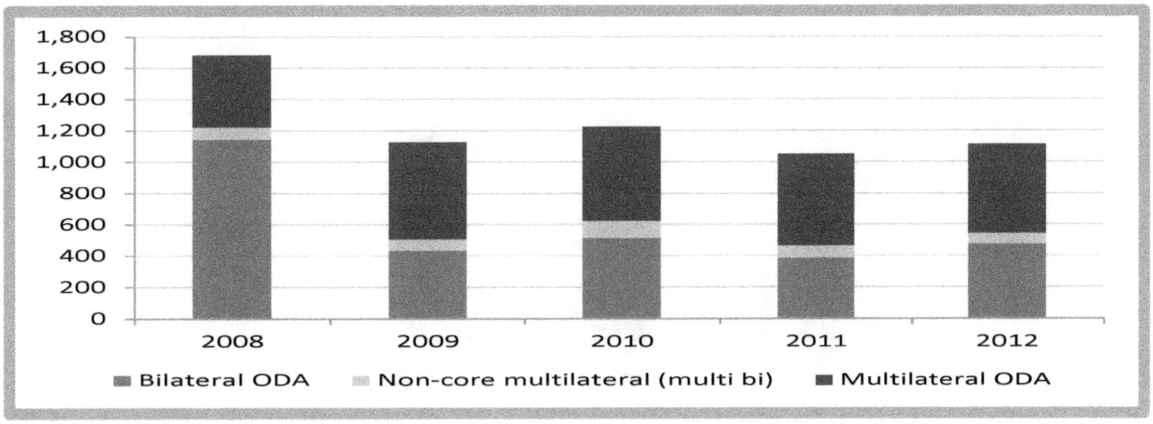

Source: DAC statistics.

Figure 3.5 Austria's contributions to multilateral trust funds

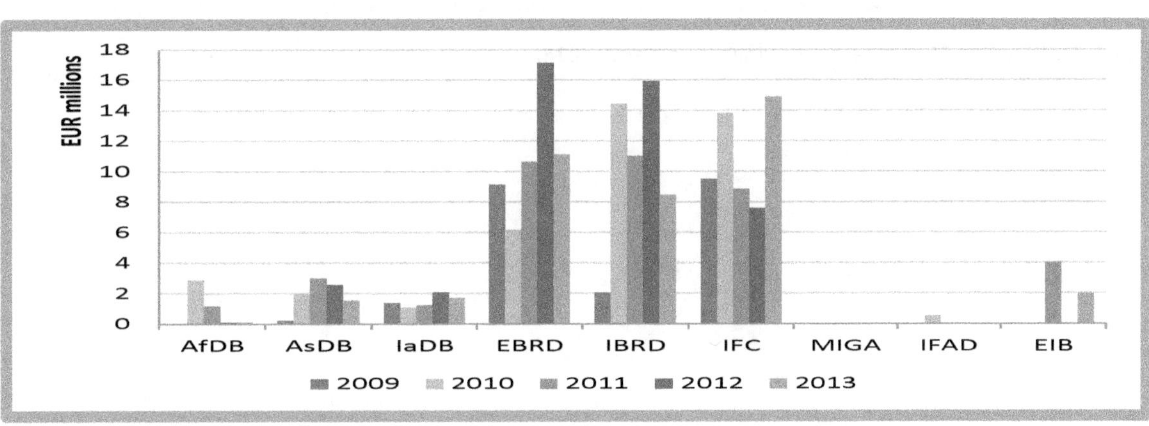

Source: Based on Ministry of Finance data.

Figure 3.6 Austria's multilateral aid, 2007-12

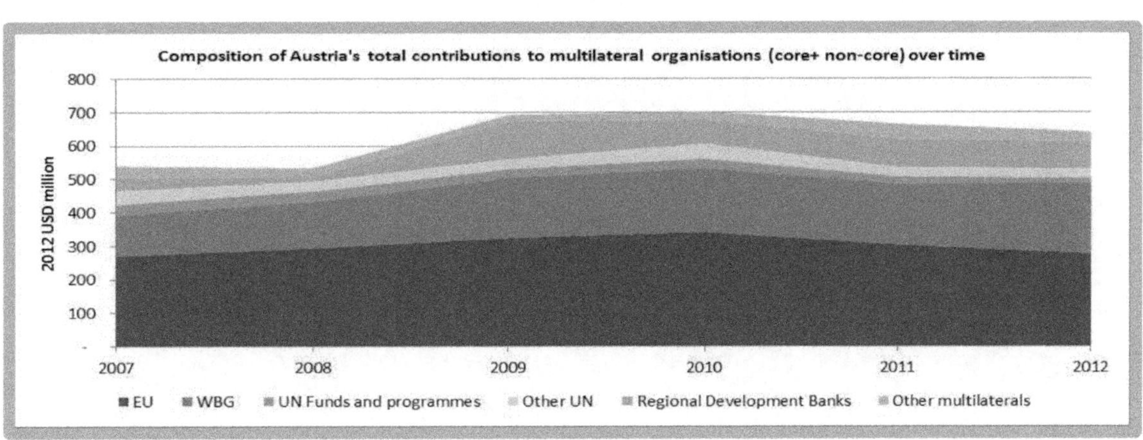

Source: OECD (forthcoming).

Figure 3.7 Austria's core contributions to UN organisations and the IUCN, 2010-14

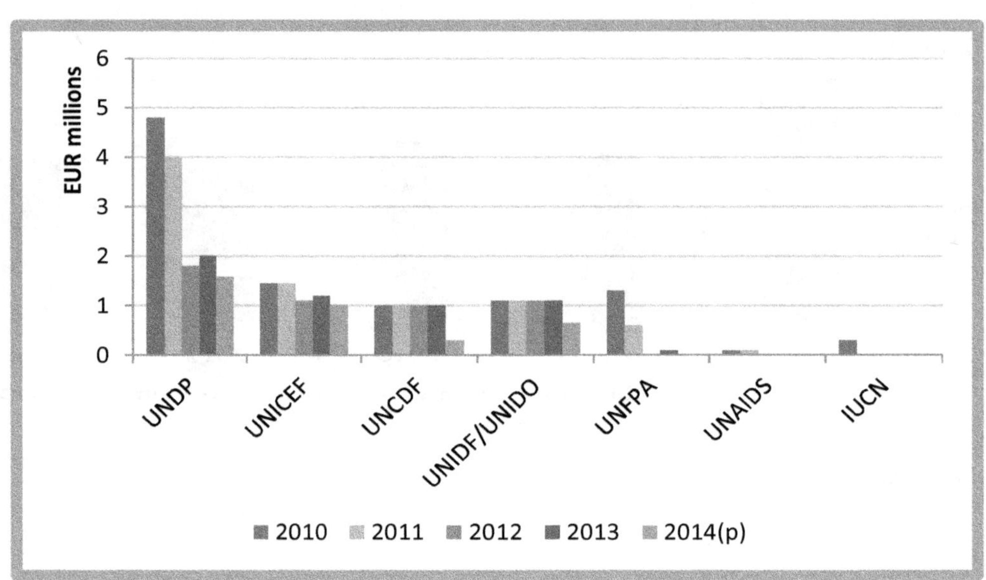

Source: Based on MFA data; p = preliminary data for 2014.

Notes

1. In 2010 the government introduced a four-year rolling budget framework covering all public expenditures. Based on this framework, budget reductions for all ministries (including reductions for the ADA and the MFA) were announced for the period until 2014.

2. In 2012 allocation to Côte d'Ivoire was particularly high due to debt relief operations.

3. To put it differently, 57% of Austrian bilateral ODA spent in 2012 (i.e. in-donor refugees costs 11%, imputed student costs 21%, debt relief 18%, administrative costs 6%, and promotion of development awareness 1.3%) did not leave Austria.

4. It includes support provided in the form of imputed student costs.

5. This figure nets out the overlaps between Rio and environment markers: it shows climate-related aid as a sub-category of total environmental aid; biodiversity and desertification are also included (either overlapping with climate-related aid, or as additional – other – environmental aid) but are not separately identified for the sake of readability of the figure.

6. According to OECD (2014), Austria has a fairly low average share of earmarked funding but higher variability (i.e. most multilateral partners receive a larger than average share of earmarked funding). In 2012 Austria provided, on average, only 19% of its total funding as earmarked resources, but most multilateral organisations funded by Austria received a share of earmarked funding above 19%. Four UN organisations (OCHA, OHCHR, UNFPA and UNICEF) received 100% earmarked funding from Austria in that year.

7. Austria's (burden) shares vis-à-vis the International Development Association (IDA) fund and the African Development Fund stand at 1.56% and 2.40% respectively (MoF data).

8. According to the Federal Ministry of Finance, Austria currently contributes to over 70 different trust funds set up in the international finance institutions: the African Development Bank (AfDB) (3); the Asian Development Bank (ADB) (7); the European Bank for Reconstruction and Development (EBRD) (11); the International Bank for Reconstruction and Development (IBRD) (19); the International Finance Corporation (IFC) (22); the Inter-American Development Bank (IaDB) (7); and the European Investment Bank (EIB) (2).

9. The MFA's UN contributions are not legally bound and are paid out of its discretionary funds. According to the MFA, the discretionary nature of its multilateral co-operation budget makes it susceptible to budget cuts.

Bibliography

Government sources

GoA (Federal Government of Austria) (2013), *Work Programme of the Austrian Federal Government 2013-2018: Austria. A Story of Success*, Austrian Federal Chancellery, Vienna, www.bka.gv.at/DocView.axd?CobId=53588.

MFA (Federal Ministry for Europe, Integration and Foreign Affairs) (2014), *OECD DAC Peer Review of Austria: Memorandum*, April 2014, MFA, Vienna.

MFA (2012), *Three Year Programme on Austrian Development Policy 2013-2015*, MFA, Vienna, www.entwicklung.at/uploads/media/ThreeYearProgramme_13-15_02.pdf.

Other sources

OECD (forthcoming), *Multilateral Aid Report 2015*, OECD Publishing, Paris.

OECD (2014), *Making Earmarked Funding More Effective: Current Practices and a Way Forward*, Report No 1, http://www.oecd.org/development/aid-architecture/Multilateral%20Report%20N%201_2014.pdf.

OECD (2009), *Austria: Development Assistance Committee (DAC) Peer Review*, OECD Publishing, Paris, http://dx.doi.org/10.1787/1996580x.

OECD/UNDP (United Nations Development Programme) (2014), *Making Development Co-operation More Effective: 2014 Progress Report*, OECD Publishing, Paris, http://dx.doi.org/10.1787/9789264209305-en.

Chapter 4: Managing Austria's development co-operation

Institutional system

Indicator: The institutional structure is conductive to consistent, quality development co-operation

As there are several government institutions involved in Austrian aid, managing the system efficiently around the objectives of the three-year programmes requires strong political will and buy-in from relevant federal ministries. The follow-up to the post-2015 sustainable development agenda offers an opportunity for the government to review the range of competencies needed to address the development challenges linked to that agenda as well as the division of labour among the different institutions involved, and to increase the coherence of the whole aid system with a view to improving the delivery of Austrian aid in partner countries.

Managing the system efficiently requires strong leadership and political will

Managing the system more efficiently around the objectives contained in the three-year programmes will require strong leadership and political will, as well as buy-in from relevant federal ministries.[1] Setting up an inclusive, structured and consistent process to engage Austrian official actors more formally in development issues would be an important step forward. Austria's Federal Ministry for Europe, Integration and Foreign Affairs (MFA) can build on the vision captured in the "mission statement," and on the three-year programmes, to raise the profile of development co-operation within the government as well as nationally.

Institutional co-ordination is a challenging task for the Ministry of Foreign Affairs

The Federal Act on Development Co-operation gives the MFA (Division VII) overall responsibility for development co-operation, including co-ordinating and formulating policy and conducting dialogue within Austria and at the international level. In reality, the MFA is one among equals and has no formal authority over other ministries, which operate independently with separate mandates and discretionary budgets. This makes the MFA's co-ordinating role a challenging task. Since the MFA manages only 4.18% of Austria's total ODA (as well as the ADA's operational and administrative budget), this ministry has little leverage. As observed in Moldova, the multiplicity of structures can translate into different instruments (including logos), processes and budget lines and generate transaction costs overall.

An analysis of the interface between the MFA and the Austrian Development Agency (ADA), carried out in 2011 by the MFA's internal oversight office, did not identify any overlaps or redundancies.[2] The ADA implements development programmes together with public institutions, NGOs and private enterprises.[3] Its operational budget has shrunk significantly, from EUR 103 million in 2008 to EUR 66 million in 2012. Further cuts are foreseen in 2015 and beyond. This situation makes medium- to long-term financial planning and programming increasingly difficult. The agency has been authorised to implement EU-financed projects with other development partners, which increases the volume of aid it manages. EU funds are channelled through indirect centralised management or twinning. This approach complies with the EU Agenda for Change and ADA's business plan and allows the agency to retain expertise.[4] At the same time, the approach puts ADA in a competitive position with other European development agencies as well as with private sector firms, making its sustainability less predictable.

This could put at risk ADA's ability to implement the official aid programme effectively.

Austria should implement a whole-of-government approach at country level

Ensuring its overall institutional structure is conducive to efficient and quality development co-operation remains challenging for Austria. The follow-up to the post-2015 sustainable development agenda is an opportunity for the government to review the range of competencies needed to address the development challenges linked to that agenda and the division of labour among the different institutions involved, and to think in terms of adopting a whole-of-government approach to its development co-operation. Implementing such an approach entails strong political leadership as well as formal co-ordination mechanisms. In this context, the MFA is encouraged to reflect on its capacity to implement the development component of its foreign policy and co-ordinate the programme across the aid system, as mandated by federal law.

An important step towards a more unified approach for improving the delivery of aid in priority partner countries would be for the main public actors of Austria's aid to agree on a set of common development objectives so that these countries can fully capitalise on the range of Austria's competencies. Follow-up steps would involve elaborating common country strategies and reporting on a single set of country results. As major operators of Austria's development co-operation, the Austrian Development Agency (ADA) and the Austrian Development Bank are well placed to build strong linkages across their respective programmes and combine their activities to meet the development priorities of Austria's partner countries. The Austrian federal government could draw on the experiences of other DAC members, for example Switzerland, where by sharing one strategy and providing complementary support to common priority countries, the Swiss Agency for Development and Cooperation (SDC) and the State Secretariat for Economic Affairs (SECO) are able to strengthen the efficiency of Swiss co-operation in these countries (OECD, 2013b). Exploring a similar avenue would contribute to increasing the development impact of Austria's aid at country level.

Austria delegates programming authority to the field; bringing the other federal ministries in line around the country strategy remains an issue

As agreed in Busan, Austria has delegated programming authority for Austrian aid to the field. While responsibility for country and regional strategies rests with the MFA, the field offices can prepare the first draft of country strategies, and "country teams" composed of representatives of the MFA, other stakeholders and the ADA (regional and thematic desks) integrate the priorities of Austrian stakeholders. However, the financial autonomy of country offices remains limited. The heads of country offices manage only a modest discretionary budget for implementing small projects.

As observed in Moldova, the head of the ADC office initiates the programming process, consulting the national and sub-national authorities as well as other development partners, as needed, and maintaining the relationship with the MFA throughout the process. The joint representation of the ADA and the MFA, under the strategic leadership of the head of the ADC office, facilitates interactions between these agencies and with the partner country and reduces the layers and levels of project approval. However, there is no formalised system for bringing the other federal ministries in line around the country strategy. The head of the ADC office solicits the expertise of line ministry attachés and consultants to the extent possible, and in response to specific needs. The review team felt there was scope for reinforcing the role of the head of the ADC office to include formal co-ordination of all Austrian actors.

The head of the ADC office reports to the Ambassador, based in Bucharest, Romania, or jointly with Bucharest to Vienna on all political matters. In many instances the head of the ADC office has reported directly to Vienna in close co-ordination with Bucharest. This contributes to Austria's visibility and role in Moldova, and strengthens the links between development and foreign policy objectives.

In Transnistria (Annex C), Austria contributes to confidence-building measures through the funding of NGO activities in the context of a regional programme of the Council of Europe.[5] Austria's flexible support allows the ADC to adapt to the evolving context there.

Innovation and behaviour change

Indicator: The system supports innovation

The Austrian Development Bank has established itself as a leader in terms of innovation, result orientation and risks management. The merge of ADA's Development Communication and Education unit and the co-financing of Austrian NGO units has resulted in improved internal communication on NGOs within ADA.

The Austrian Development Bank is a driver in terms of innovation

The most important change since the last peer review is the growth of the Austrian Development Bank and the creation of an adequate organisational structure fit for purpose. As discussed in Chapter 1, the Bank's mandate is to be a catalyst to promote private investment in order to support development efforts in partner countries. Its activities could be better interlinked with ADA's activities in the same sector. The Bank has introduced a result orientation in its operations and manages fiduciary risks. This is considered good practice.

Following the 2013 elections and the appointment of a new minister, the MFA gained a new competency for "integration" and its name was changed to the Federal Ministry for Europe, Integration and Foreign Affairs. The ADA's Development Communication and Education unit and the co-financing of Austrian NGO units were merged in 2011, primarily to pool responsibilities for co-operating with these actors and indicate to them that they were key ADC players. The review team was informed that Austrian NGOs have appreciated this merger, which has also resulted in improved internal communication on NGOs within ADA.

Human resources

Indicator: The member manages its human resources effectively to respond to field imperatives

Managing human resources remains a challenge for Austria's development co-operation. Recognising development co-operation as a career path within the MFA and ensuring that the right skills are in the right places, including for dealing with fragile contexts, would be significant steps forward. Further budget constraints may prevent the ADA from recruiting the external technical expertise needed to implement its programme, and hamper knowledge building and continuity.

Managing human resources and ensuring the right skills are in the right places remain challenging

The 2009 peer review (OECD, 2009) urged Austria to ensure that Division VII of the MFA had the required resources to set development co-operation policy, give strategic directions, monitor and evaluate, and report on results. The emphasis on the environment and on relations with the EU has been strengthened since the last peer review, reflecting the strategic priorities of the Three-Year Programme and enabling Division VII to play an active role in multilateral fora.[6] The division has maintained a staff of 31 (2014) despite decreasing administrative budgets in the Austrian public sector (Annex D). Of these, 11 are diplomats and 10 are development experts.[7] The number of development experts is likely to shrink, with several retirements upcoming and no plans for replacing these experts.

The MFA may face a difficult task with respect to guiding development co-operation, particularly in sectoral and thematic areas where other federal entities have expertise relevant to international co-operation. Special arrangements to ensure that staff members with the appropriate skills are deployed to fragile contexts are also lacking in both the ministry and the agency. Staff exchanges and rotations with other organisations, including other federal ministries, are rare. Recognising development co-operation as a career path within the MFA, and ensuring that the ministry has the required expertise to continue providing strategic direction and that there is more permeability between institutions, would be significant steps forward.

Figure 4.1 Human resources in Austria's development co-operation (2009 and 2013)

				2009	2013
Institution	**Type of staff**			**No. of posts filled**	**No. of posts filled**
MFA	**Experts and diplomats**			**21**	**22**
	Trainees			**2**	**3**
	Support			**10**	**8**
ADA	**Experts**	**Headquarters (HQ)**		**87**	**83**
		Field offices	**From HQ**	**23**	**16**
			Locally recruited	**52**	**45**
		Other missions		**-**	**2**
MoF	**Financial experts**	**HQ**		**10**	**10**
		Representation at IFIs		**6**	**5**
Austrian Development Bank	**Experts (e.g. financial, legal, risk)**			**11**	**29**
	Support			**2**	**3**
Total				**224**	**226**

Source: MFA (2014).

Being the main provider of development expertise within the Austrian development co-operation system has not prevented the ADA from experiencing staff reductions (Figure 4.1). Austria reports that cuts were driven by the reduction in the number of priority countries and took place primarily through attrition rather than lay-offs. Currently staff at headquarters and in the field together administer over 500 projects using many different instruments, quite a large number given the size of the agency's core aid budget (Chapter 3). Most thematic areas and country desks are manned by one person, stretching the agency's administrative resources to the limit. Staff constraints are also felt in the Quality Assurance and Knowledge Management Unit dealing with sectoral priorities and cross-cutting issues (Chapter 2). The ADA depends on locally recruited experts, as well as NGOs, to make project proposals and implement these projects in priority countries. Further budget cuts could prevent the ADA from recruiting the external technical expertise needed to deliver its programme, and hamper knowledge building and continuity.

Other important government actors, such as the Federal Ministry of Finance and the Austrian Development Bank, have not been affected by staff reductions in recent years. The Bank's growing activities have led to the recruitment of 19 new staff, reflecting its ability to extend its operations (Chapter 1).

The ADA has a flexible personnel policy, but training and learning need to be given higher priority

The 2009 peer review (OECD, 2009) recommended the ADA's staff development strategy be complemented by personnel policies that provide a clear explanation of how job rotations and exchanges work, and address locally recruited staff. It appears that the agency's personnel policy does not specifically address these aspects of human resources management. Nevertheless, the policy is rather flexible and offers attractive conditions to qualified technical staff hired locally. In Moldova, for example, the head of the ADC office has a four-year contract (renewable once in the same country), can rotate between different field offices, and can eventually be integrated into the ADA's headquarters provided a permanent position can be found there. This option is somewhat limited by the small number of posts available. The terms of employment of local staff follow the rules and regulations of their country.

The ADA does not have a specific training plan for its staff. Nevertheless, it organises some training, including for locally recruited staff and occasionally MFA staff, in a limited number of areas (e.g. languages, accounting, law, project cycle management and project finance management). The agency is a member of "learn4dev" and thus has access to training programmes through this competence development network. In Moldova the budget dedicated to training local staff is limited to EUR 2 000 for the whole office. This training can take place in Vienna or neighbouring countries. There is scope for the ADA to invest further in developing staff competencies at headquarters and field level. The ADA could give greater priority to training and on-the-job learning, including on cross-cutting themes, by putting in place a training plan that is adequately resourced and is linked to its staff performance management system.

Notes

1. Besides the MFA, six federal ministries are involved in managing Austrian development co-operation (Finance; Agriculture, Forestry, Environment and Water Management; Defence and Sports; Interior; Education and Women's Affairs; and Arts and Culture, Constitution and Media) in addition to the Austrian Development Agency and the Austrian Development Bank, both of which implement Austrian aid.

2. The MFA's report on "Sektion VII – Schnittstellenprüfung" is an internal audit report with restricted access.

3. The ADA was created on 1 January 2004 as a non-profit company "to prepare and implement measures of development co-operation [with] particular attention being paid to their effectiveness in developing countries" (GoA, 2003). The last peer review observed that the role and responsibilities of the ADA and the MFA needed to be clarified (OECD, 2009).

4. In 2014 estimated disbursements in the context of implementation of EU projects amounted to EUR 17.6 million. At this stage, these projects run from 2009 to 2018 and are implemented in Albania, Central America, Moldova and Uganda (a total volume of EUR 61.25 million).

5. In 2010-12 the Council of Europe's confidence-building programmes covered the areas of education, children's rights and the rights of people with disabilities; civil society; media; inter-municipal co-operation; and drugs control. Since then, new areas include good governance; cultural heritage rehabilitation; trafficking in human beings; and human rights training for the legal professions.

6. A new unit (Unit VII.3a) for "Environment and Sustainability" (one staff member) facilitates the MFA's co-operation with the ADA's environment and natural resources unit (two staff members) and the Federal Ministry of Agriculture, Forestry, Environment and Water Management. Unit VII.5d is dedicated to planning and programming EU funds (one staff member), while Unit VII.1a (one staff member) is responsible for co-ordinating and formulating Austria's position on the EU Council Working Party on Development Cooperation (CODEV).

7. The 11 diplomats include the director general, 4 directors, 2 heads of units and 4 task managers. The development experts include 1 director, 6 heads of units and 3 task managers.

Bibliography

Government sources

ADA (Austrian Development Agency) (2013), *Bhutan Country Strategy 2010-2013: Austrian Development Cooperation,* ADA, Vienna, www.entwicklung.at/uploads/media/CS_Bhutan_2010-2013_July2011_03.pdf.

GoA (Federal Government of Austria) (2003), *Federal Act on Development Cooperation (2002), Including its Amendment (2003)*, GoA, Vienna, www.entwicklung.at/uploads/media/development_cooperation_law_01.pdf.

MFA (Federal Ministry for Europe, Integration and Foreign Affairs) (2014), *DAC Peer Review of Austria: Memorandum*, MFA, Vienna.

MFA (2013), *Mid-Term Review Report*, MFA, Vienna.

MFA (2012a), *Three Year Programme on Austrian Development Policy 2013-2015*, MFA, Vienna, www.entwicklung.at/uploads/media/ThreeYearProgramme_13-15.pdf.

MFA (2012b), *Foreign and European Policy Report 2012 – Report by the Federal Minister for European and International Affairs*, MFA, Vienna, www.bmeia.gv.at/en/the-ministry/foreign-and-european-policy-report/.

MFA (2011a), *Sektion VII – Schnittstellenprüfung*, internal MFA report, December 2011, Inspector General, MFA, Vienna.

MFA (2011b), *Security and Development in Austrian Development Policy: Strategic Guideline*, MFA, Vienna, www.entwicklung.at/uploads/media/StratGuide_Security_and_Development.pdf.

MFA (2010), *Three-Year Programme on Austrian Development Policy 2010-2012. Revised Version 2010*, MFA, Vienna, www.entwicklung.at/uploads/media/Three-YearProgramme10-12_03.pdf.

Other sources

OECD (2013a), *Decentralisation of DAC Members' Development Co-operation Systems*, DCD (2013)7, OECD, Paris.

OECD (2013b), *Switzerland: Development Assistance Committee (DAC) Peer Review*, OECD Publishing, Paris, http://dx.doi.org/10.1787/9789264196322-en.

OECD (2009), *Austria: Development Assistance Committee (DAC) Peer Review,* OECD Publishing, Paris, http://dx.doi.org/10.1787/1996580x.

Chapter 5: Austria's development co-operation delivery and partnerships

Budgeting and programming processes

Indicator: These processes support quality aid as defined in Busan

Austria communicates indicative spending plans to only three priority countries. It could extend the provision of similar information to all priority countries. Currently, aid predictability with respect to other partner governments appears to be insufficient.

Austria's multi-year ODA forecast contributes to aid predictability, but greater effort is needed at country level

Austria has worked to make its development co-operation more predictable since the last peer review. For example, it adopted a multi-year ODA forecast for the period 2011-14, which is updated annually in line with the rolling four-year national budget framework introduced in 2010. The in-year predictability of Austrian aid has also improved: in 2013 Austria disbursed 94% of its aid in keeping with the agreed schedules (OECD/UNDP, 2014).[1]

Aid predictability at country level remains partial, however. Austria formally communicates indicative spending plans to only three of its priority countries (Bhutan, Burkina Faso and Ethiopia), with which it signed multi-annual co-operation agreements.[2] While Austria shares such forward spending plans with other priority countries informally and upon their request, extending the provision of similar information more officially and consistently to all priority countries would help enhance their ability to plan.

In Moldova the ADC office provides indicative future spending for specific programmes or projects that run over several years. However, the office is not in a position to give the Moldovan government a consolidated view of the funding the government can expect from Austria, as it only has limited knowledge of aid flows related to the activities administered by other ministries. Austria is encouraged to make progress on aid predictability in all its priority countries.

Austria's aid is aligned to partner country strategies

Austria is beginning to use new ways to deliver its aid programme, including delegated co-operation, joint programming, and new tools for engaging with the private sector. Its support is aligned to partner country strategies and draws upon its own experience. Programming at country level is guided by medium-term country strategies or co-operation agreements and by the Three-Year Programme 2013-2015. Austria's approach to identifying projects in close dialogue with its local partners has helped ensure alignment. Its activities in Moldova demonstrate its ability to align with the priorities of a partner government's strategic documents.

Awareness of aid effectiveness principles is high; more effort is needed to increase use of country systems

Awareness of aid effectiveness principles (Paris, Accra and Busan) is high among Austrian ODA actors. As the review team observed in Moldova, Austria has made progress in implementing a number of aid effectiveness principles. It aligns with its partner countries' national priorities and makes use of their institutions and systems to varying degrees, depending on the country context. Ownership is promoted at national and sub-national levels. In Moldova, for example, the ADC office has sufficiently decentralised authority and flexibility to respond to evolving country needs. The field office co-operates closely with local institutions and stakeholders, and delivers some aspects of its water supply programme using local procurement.

More efforts are needed to increase the use of country systems wherever possible. The 2014 Global Partnership monitoring survey found that only 21% of Austria's scheduled aid flows to governments were recorded in partner countries' budgets (OECD/UNDP, 2014). Project-based assistance continues to be Austria's preferred approach for delivering aid. In line with the Busan commitment, where country systems are not robust Austria could also work with the partner government and other external stakeholders to identify the weaknesses of, and build capacity in, country systems.

Austria developed an Accra Agenda for Action implementation plan in the run-up to the Busan High Level Forum, and participated actively in formulating the Busan agenda. It is encouraged to make use of and continue to actively participate in global discussions on development effectiveness. More efforts to implement the commitments, and enhanced engagement in the Global Partnership for Effective Development Co-operation, could increase the quality of Austrian development co-operation and its contribution to achieve development results.

Austria's programme lacks a systematic approach to risk management

Risk is analysed in some aspects of Austrian development co-operation. For example, the Austrian Development Bank actively manages risks in its programmes. The expected development impact of investment projects financed by the Bank is systematically assessed by an inter-ministerial Business and Development Board.[3] The risk dimension of these projects is also assessed by the Advisory Council. However, there does not appear to be a comprehensive risk assessment and management process in Austria's overall aid (ADC) strategy: how major risks to the success of its overall development portfolio are identified, analysed, managed and monitored is not clear.

In Moldova, while Austria takes a sufficiently systematic approach to risks in its activities in the breakaway region of Transnistria, the ADC office in Chisinau does not appear to receive adequate guidance from headquarters to take a comprehensive approach to risks throughout the country programme. Staff are left to decide the best ways to incorporate risk management into programming; this means the overall aid portfolio, and Austria's aid institutions, could be exposed to significant unmanaged threats.

Where fiduciary risks are concerned, Austria places high priority on anti-corruption. It adheres to the 1996 DAC recommendation on anti-corruption and is a State party to the OECD Anti-Bribery Convention. For example, the ADA's General Terms and Conditions for Grants provide conditions under which recipients shall be obliged to immediately repay any funds already disbursed, and entitlements to undisbursed funds shall expire. The provisions in the agency's agreement on general budget support for a developing country "reserve the right of ADA to withhold and/or reclaim all or parts of the grant in case of misappropriation or misuse of funds" (MFA, 2014). While the agency does not routinely check debarment lists of multilateral financial institutions, it routinely verifies the reliability of potential project partners, including their degree of creditworthiness (OECD, 2012). There is scope for further improvement. According to the most recent evaluation of Austria's implementation of the Anti-Bribery Convention, there is not a high level of awareness in the Austrian administration of the appropriate channels for making reports on bribery of foreign public officials in relation to ODA contracting (OECD, 2012).

The share of untied aid has fallen below the DAC average

Traditionally, the share of Austrian aid that is untied has been boosted by high levels of debt forgiveness which, by convention, is regarded as untied aid. Even with this debt forgiveness, however, Austria's untying performance has been well below the DAC average. With respect to ODA covered by the Untying Recommendation (i.e. ODA which should be 100% untied), the share untied by Austria fell from 95% in 2010 to 77% in 2012, well below the DAC average of 88%. Concerning total bilateral ODA (excluding administrative costs and in-donor refugee costs), overall untying fell even more dramatically, from 58% in 2010 to 37% in 2012, whereas the DAC average (78% in 2012) has held up well since Accra and despite the global economic and financial crisis. In that connection, Austria was one of few countries which did not meet the Accra commitment to provide a clear plan for untying a significant share of remaining tied aid.

Austria does not attach conditions

Austria negotiates agreements with partners in a transparent way and does not appear to attach any specific conditions, other than mutually agreed performance results and reporting requirements. In Moldova conditionality did not appear to be an issue, including for soft loans.

Partnerships

Indicator: The member makes appropriate use of co-ordination arrangements, promotes strategic partnerships to develop synergies, and enhances mutual accountability

Austria works in line with the EU framework and actively supports the EU Code of Conduct on Division of Labour. The programme in Moldova clearly demonstrates Austria's ability to identify opportunities for delegated co-operation in line with the EU Agenda for Change. While NGOs play an important role in Austrian aid as development partners, Austria could be more strategic in engaging with partner country civil society and set clear engagement policy or objectives at both strategic and delivery levels.

Austria is a team player and actively engages in joint work

Austria actively supports and engages in donor co-ordination in the field. It is also fully committed to, and works in line with, the EU framework and actively supports the EU Code of Conduct on the Division of Labour. For example, in Moldova it takes the lead in the water and sanitation operations in the Nisporeni district. Austria also uses delegated co-operation and silent partnerships as means of increasing aid effectiveness and reducing transaction costs in the long term. The programme in Moldova clearly demonstrates Austria's ability to identify opportunities for delegated co-operation in line with the EU Agenda for Change. This is also a clear objective in the ADA's business model.

Austria engages with other development partners in a number of activities, which contributes to scaling up development outcomes. In Moldova, for example, it is widely viewed by other development partners as a good team player, supporting and promoting co-ordination with and among the government and partners at the operational level. It actively supports and takes the lead in relevant co-ordination platforms and joint funding mechanisms. The ADC office decides, in consultation with the ADA (and the MFA), which partnerships are best able to implement the country programme.

This approach appears to result in strategic and well-tailored partnerships.

Austria engages in mutual accountability mechanisms where they exist

Austria reports that it supports and promotes mutual accountability in partner countries where there are sound foundations in place.[4] For example, it engages in joint frameworks and uses partner countries' own results frameworks as benchmarks for monitoring its country programmes in Ethiopia, Mozambique and Uganda (MFA, 2014). In Moldova, Austria adheres to the government-donors Partnership Principles Implementation Plan (Annex C).

NGOs are important development partners; a more strategic approach is needed

Austria has a clear policy of engagement with Austrian NGOs, outlined in its 2007 NGO co-operation guidelines. NGOs play an important role in its development co-operation as development partners implementing ADA-funded projects and programmes. Around 40% of the ADA's annual operating budget is implemented by Austrian, local and international NGOs, either through co-financing arrangements or directly. Since the last peer review, Austria has taken actions to reduce transaction costs associated with the financing of Austrian NGOs and provide more predictability and flexibility to these partners. The multi-annual NGO Framework Programmes enable it to engage with Austrian NGOs over the medium to long term. Austria could do more to ensure all frameworks are built around result-oriented programmes, as recommended in 2009.

While Austria's NGO policy includes strengthening partner country NGOs as a key objective, there is still room for improvement. In Moldova, for example, Austria's financing of and engagement with Moldovan grassroots organisations and NGOs are considered important aspects of its country programme. While local NGOs appreciate Austrian support and efforts to sustain relationships with them, they are not consulted on Austria's strategy and programming, and dialogue is limited. In addition, for small amounts of funding there appear to be high transaction costs for local NGOs. There is scope for reducing and further simplifying administrative requirements, as well as procedures for funding and reporting. Austria might consider updating its NGO co-operation guidelines to set clear policy or strategic objectives to guide Austria's engagement with partner country civil society at both strategic and delivery levels.

Fragile states

Indicator: Delivery modalities and partnerships help ensure quality

Austria is committed to the Fragile States Principles, but does not yet consistently apply a fragility lens in designing programmes for these difficult contexts. Reducing the scope of its priorities for peacebuilding and statebuilding to be more realistic could be a useful next step. Partnership with civil society actors in these contexts is a useful approach; this is good practice, given that most fragility programmes are delivered through partners and multi-donor trust funds. Austria also makes a significant contribution to peacebuilding efforts.

A fragility lens is not yet consistently applied for programming in these difficult contexts

Austria does not yet consistently apply a fragility lens for programming in these complex and constantly changing contexts. Country strategies can be developed by field staff without seeking any input from fragility experts (e.g. in Burkina Faso). As Austria anticipates updating its security and development guidelines, it would be useful to consider how it will work towards achieving its peacebuilding and statebuilding goals, including how to identify trade-offs and dilemmas, weigh short- versus long-term effects, and be realistic about what can be achieved within a given timeframe.

Austria co-ordinates with other actors in fragile contexts

Austria engages with multi-donor trust funds to increase coherence in fragile contexts, including pooled funding arrangements with Denmark and Sweden to support the African Union, the Economic Community of Western African States (ECOWAS) and the Intergovernmental Authority on Development (IGAD) interventions in fragile contexts (MFA, 2014). It also contributes troops to peacekeeping missions – 905 were deployed as of June 2014, the majority to Bosnia and Herzegovina, Kosovo and Lebanon.

Mostly working through partners in fragile contexts

Austria works mostly with multilateral and NGO partners in such contexts. It does not have sufficiently flexible funding tools to allow it to work bilaterally in most of these difficult environments. Therefore, it has developed principles for how partners should work together in fragile contexts; this was done through the Vienna 3C Appeal (GoA et al., 2010), which brought together various government and civil society actors to set out the 16 principles and the aims of acting together.

Notes

1. The figure is calculated on the basis of a sample of partner countries reported by Austria to the monitoring exercise (country programmable aid worth USD 44 million) and thus does not represent its full country programmable aid portfolio (which amounted to USD 65 million).

2. However, the information contained in these indicative spending plans remains partial as they cover ADC funds only and not all Austrian ODA flows.

3. The developmental effects of all Austrian Development Bank's investment projects are assessed against four criteria (development impact; the particular strategic role of the Bank; the project's long-term profitability; its contribution to the Bank's expected return) using the Corporate Policy Project Rating Tool (GPR). The projects are scored on a scale from 1 (very good) to 6 (obviously insufficient). The average GPR score for the Bank's projects in 2013 was 1.8.

4. Austria supports "joint programming" as an effective way to promote mutual accountability and ensure coherence. This approach foresees the elaboration (together with the host partner country) of a single country strategy, whose implementation is then divided among the participating donor countries in order to avoid overlaps and duplications, thus contributing to coherent implementation of development activities at country level (OECD, 2014).

Bibliography

Government sources

GoA (Federal Government of Austria) et al. (2010), *Vienna 3C Appeal: Co-ordinated, Complementary and Coherent Measures in Fragile Situations. Principles and Aims of Interaction between Government and Non-Governmental Actors. Recommendations*, Vienna, www.entwicklung.at/uploads/media/Vienna_3C_Appeal.pdf.

MFA (Federal Ministry for Europe, Integration and Foreign Affairs) (2014), *OECD DAC Peer Review of Austria: Memorandum*, April 2014, MFA, Vienna.

MFA (2012), *Three Year Programme on Austrian Development Policy 2013-2015*, MFA, Vienna, www.entwicklung.at/uploads/media/ThreeYearProgramme_13-15_02.pdf.

Other sources

OECD (2014), *Better Policies for Development 2014: Policy Coherence and Illicit Financial Flows*, OECD Publishing, Paris, http://dx.doi.org/10.1787/9789264210325-en.

OECD (2012), *Phase 3 Report on Implementing the OECD Antir-Bribery Convention in Austria*, OECD Publishing, Paris, www.oecd.org/daf/anti-bribery/austria-oecdanti-briberyconvention.htm.

OECD (2009), *Austria: Development Assistance Committee (DAC) Peer Review*, OECD Publishing, Paris, http://dx.doi.org/10.1787/1996580x.

OECD (2007), *Principles for Good International Engagement in Fragile States and Situations*, OECD Publishing, Paris, www.oecd.org/development/incaf/38368714.pdf.

OECD/UNDP (United Nations Development Programme) (2014), *Making Development Co-operation More Effective: 2014 Progress Report*, OECD Publishing, Paris, http://dx.doi.org/10.1787/9789264209305-en.

Chapter 6: Results management and accountability of Austria's development co-operation

Results-based management system

Indicator: A results-based management system is in place to assess performance on the basis of development priorities, objectives and systems of partner countries

Austria has taken a number of positive steps in favour of managing for results. It still lacks a consistent and coherent approach, as well as a vision of how results are used to inform decisions and demonstrate accountability. Results efforts are at different stages of development at the project, country and corporate levels. There are no linkages between them, or with the development objectives of the Three-Year Programme. Neither is there a differentiated approach to setting out, monitoring or reporting expected results in fragile contexts. Austria is beginning to use the country data and results systems of its partner countries. This practice needs to be systematised, as Austria further develops results frameworks for all its country programmes.

Austria has taken steps to build results into programming, but a coherent and consistent approach is still needed

The Austrian federal government is currently introducing result-based management principles for the entire Austrian administration. For example, as an integral part of preparing the 2013 and 2014 budgets, the MFA defined results and indicators for development co-operation, with the obligation to report against these indicators. This orientation, combined with the 2009 peer review recommendation asking Austria to develop a culture of managing for results for its aid system, have led to a number of positive steps, such as:

- The Three-Year Programme 2013-2015 includes a results matrix, with expected outcomes for the sectors and themes of Austria's priority countries and regions.
- The new format of country strategies also includes output and outcome indicators aligned with the priorities of partner countries.
- Results-based management approaches are being introduced in ADC's NGO funding guidelines, applications and reporting.
- Dedicated training and experience-sharing workshops and presentations by peers – such as the Swiss Agency for Development and Cooperation (SDC) and the Swedish International Development Cooperation Agency (Sida) – have been organised for staff at headquarters and at field level (e.g. in Uganda).

Moreover, the Federal Ministry of Finance (MoF) advocates the use of results frameworks and corporate scorecards for the IFIs, and requires project-specific results frameworks in multi-bi programmes co-funded by Austria. At the Austrian Development Bank, results are measured using a rigorous and comprehensive framework developed in close consultation with MoF.

While these efforts are significant, Austrian Development Cooperation (ADC) still lacks a consistent and coherent approach to development results and the results reporting process, as well as a vision of how results information can be used to inform decisions and demonstrate accountability. Results efforts are at different stages of development at the project, country and corporate levels, with no linkages between them or with the development objectives of the Three-Year Programme. At this stage, only a few country strategies have a result orientation, and only in rare cases has Austria designated benchmarks and baselines. The ADA adapted its country programme results framework to newly defined national results. Like other DAC members, Austria is challenged by the difficulty of selecting appropriate indicators that measure results at the right level, linking these results to strategic institutional goals and budget, and building a culture of learning and accountability based on good/bad practice.

Austria is beginning to use country data and results systems

Austria is aware of the need to rely on partner countries' own data and results systems for its decision-making and programming. The lack of available and reliable data in priority countries, and the difficulty of establishing a baseline, can be challenging. In Ethiopia, Mozambique and Uganda, Austria relies almost exclusively on existing national monitoring frameworks related to these strategies, which is positive. In Moldova, the results framework of Austria's country strategy has been adapted to the new national planning. These efforts need to be systematised as Austria further develops results frameworks for all its country programmes.

There is no differentiated approach for fragile contexts

Austria does not have a differentiated approach to setting out, monitoring or reporting expected results in fragile contexts. Projects are designed as stand-alone, quick-impact interventions with short-term timeframes. It is unclear how these projects take conflict sensitivity or "do no harm" approaches into account. As it strengthens its results-based management frameworks, Austria needs to ensure that they support learning and accountability in difficult contexts.

Evaluation system

Indicator: The evaluation system is in line with the DAC evaluation principles

The guidelines for project and programme evaluations follow the DAC principles, a structure with a dedicated budget is in place at the ADA, and evaluations are conducted by external consultants and made public. However, the MFA's policy evaluation capacity remains limited. The evaluation process is structurally independent of the programming and delivery of Austrian aid. An evaluation policy for the entire aid system would go a long way towards strengthening the evaluation culture of Austrian Development Cooperation. The inclusion of national experts in project evaluation teams contributes to strengthening national capacity in this area.

Evaluation guidelines and a structure are in place at the ADA; the MFA's resources are limited

The Guidelines for Project and Programme Evaluations (ADA, 2008), which are the main point of reference for all ADC evaluations, explicitly adopt the DAC Principles for Evaluation Development Assistance.[1] The Austrian Development Bank conducts its own evaluations, using the DAC guidelines as a reference and benefiting from the ADA's evaluation know-how. The other government actors involved in Austrian aid do not have separate evaluation departments or specific evaluation guidelines. Whether and how they evaluate is unclear. The review team was informed that the MFA intends to update its 2005 evaluation policy for Austria's development co-operation. An evaluation policy for the whole aid system would go a long way towards strengthening the evaluation culture of Austria's development co-operation programme.

Evaluation is an integral part of quality assurance at the ADA. The agency has a unit with two staff dedicated to evaluation whose role and responsibilities are clear. The unit manages the evaluation of projects and programmes and conducts evaluation training for staff and NGOs, as needed. It shares responsibility for strategic evaluations of country programmes and reviews, instruments and sectors/themes with the MFA. Representatives of the ADA and the MFA meet regularly to discuss and monitor the implementation of on-going evaluations/reviews and feedback processes of evaluation recommendations. With only one staff member located in the Quality Management and Evaluation Unit (VII.2.a) and no budget, the MFA's capacity is limited and the ministry relies extensively on the ADA.

The evaluation process is independent

The evaluation process is institutionally independent from the programming and delivery of Austrian development assistance, and Austria uses the DAC's Quality Standards for Development Evaluation.[2] Strategic evaluations and projects/programme evaluations are conducted by external consultants to guarantee their independence. The ADA's evaluation unit is operationally independent, reporting to the Managing Director; within the MFA, the Head of the Development Policy, Strategy and Evaluation Division (VII.2) reports to the Director General of the Development Co-operation Department (VII).

An evaluation plan with a flexible budget is available at the ADA

The ADA and the MFA develop a joint two-year evaluation plan for strategic evaluations, and a budget in line with this plan is made available on an annual basis. This budget fluctuates between EUR 300 000 and EUR 500 000, depending on the plan. The evaluation units elaborate the plan together on the basis of suggestions from other departments and units at the ADA and the MFA. The criteria for selecting strategic evaluations include having a good mix of and balance between country strategies, instruments and themes, and responding to priorities (e.g. the mid-term review of a country strategy). Capacity constraints prevent Austria from participating in joint evaluations (MFA, 2014). While joint evaluations may consume more time and human resources than ordinary evaluations, Austria's engagement in joint programming should lead it to participate more in joint evaluations. Austria should consider these processes an opportunity to learn and to reduce transaction costs for partner countries.

National counterparts are consulted

In Moldova, counterparts are consulted throughout the evaluation process and project evaluations are planned together, whether they are implemented by multilateral organisations, NGOs or the partner country's sub-national authorities. The head of the ADC office in Chisinau may propose to headquarters to conduct a review of Austria's current country programme to prepare for the next programme. The agency is therefore encouraged to identify clear criteria to guide this process. Austria includes national experts in project evaluation teams. It is encouraged to continue to support country-led efforts in this area.

Institutional learning

Indicator: Evaluation and appropriate knowledge management systems are used as management tools

Austria has established a process for evaluation reports. It still needs to ensure that senior managers follow up on recommendations from these reports, so that evaluations effectively inform strategic decisions and can be used as a management tool. Setting up an evaluation committee under the ADA's Supervisory Board could generate more commitment at all levels. Austria's new knowledge management system could support these efforts by collecting and processing lessons and experiences.

Getting senior managers to follow up on recommendations is a challenge

The last peer review noted that Austria did not have a well-defined process for feeding the outcomes of evaluations back into operations. The ADA has since developed a management response system for strategic evaluations in the form of an internal matrix, tracking recommendations and corresponding actions to be taken. The matrix is updated annually. Recommendations from evaluations are discussed with relevant staff from the ADA and the MFA, as well as with larger audiences when appropriate (e.g. NGOs in the case of CSO evaluations) and the heads of country offices during ADC's annual meetings. They are presented to senior management at both the ADA and the MFA. While these steps are encouraging, the challenge for Austria is to get senior management to ensure that findings are acted upon, so that evaluations effectively inform strategic decisions and are used as a forward-looking management tool.

In order to obtain greater commitment at all levels to follow up on the implementation of recommendations, setting up an evaluation committee under an independent oversight body like the ADA's Supervisory Board could be effective. Informing the MFA's political level about how evaluation results are implemented would also be useful.

Austria disseminates evaluation results

Austria systematically disseminates evaluation results. Final evaluation reports are sent to headquarters, and are made available on the ADC's homepage with a summary, as well as through the DAC Evaluation Resource Centre (DEReC).[3] They are shared with local counterparts, implementing entities and other relevant stakeholders in partner countries. These efforts can be built on to strengthen learning and knowledge management throughout Austria's development co-operation. Organising an "evaluation day" and/or elaborating thematic reports on findings and lessons from evaluations could be useful next steps.

An effective knowledge management system is not yet in place

The 2009 peer review noted that Austria's informal approach to knowledge management left little opportunity to document best practices and share lessons among country offices and beyond (OECD, 2009). The ADA's new knowledge management strategy, dedicated core team and action plan are important steps towards a more structured and institutionalised system. At this stage, however, efforts have focused primarily on the ADA's organisation and management processes through mapping knowledge, elaborating rules for managing knowledge assets, and integrating knowledge goals into the ADA's business plan. They do not yet capture and process lessons in a systematic way.

At field level, country offices provide information that feeds into the ADC's annual reports on development aid. As observed in Moldova, project information is also put into a database. However, the country office does not have the resources and time to organise and capitalise on this information. The sharing of experience is therefore limited. Outmoded technology and systems for managing information appear to constitute a bottleneck. The ADA is currently merging its existing databases and piloting the use of social media tools to ensure a better flow of information within the organisation. Putting in place an effective information management system capable of collecting good and bad practice among ADC country offices and partners, and sharing experiences through different fora and technologies (e.g. communities of practice, thematic networks, workshops, social media) would contribute to building a culture of knowledge and learning. In doing this, Austria should be guided by the overall objective of enabling key stakeholders to learn about what works or does not work, and why.

The Austrian Development Bank's experience provides a good illustration of institutional learning based on recommendations from an external evaluation (Box 6.1).

Box 6.1 Institutional learning within the Austrian Development Bank

Austria's Federal Ministry of Finance (MoF) has transformed the recommendations of the external evaluation of the Austrian Development Bank into an action plan discussed with major stakeholders (i.e. the ADA, the MFA and Austria's export credit agency). The action plan has led to a number of adaptations in the governance structure of the Bank. The Bank's strategy for 2013-17 provides a major instrument for feeding many recommendations back into its operations. The strategy has been discussed extensively with representatives of the MoF and the MFA, as well as the Bank's supervisory board.

Source: MFA (2014).

Communication, accountability, and development awareness

Indicator: The member communicates development results transparently and honestly

Austria has taken a number of steps to achieve aid transparency. However, it still falls short of the commitment it made in Busan. Austria performs well on sharing organisation-level information, but does not sufficiently communicate on development results and risks. The domestic accountability of its development co-operation programme is also weak. A comprehensive database of ODA allocations, covering all official assistance managed at national and sub-national levels, would contribute to improving aid transparency. Austria's approach to communication and development education has been reinforced with a strategy and dedicated budgets. It works with civil society actors to raise development awareness, but could do more to reach out to civil society beyond traditional Austrian actors.

Austria falls short of its aid transparency commitment

Austria performs well on sharing organisation-level information, but does not sufficiently communicate on development results and risks. A comprehensive database of ODA allocations, covering all official assistance managed at national and sub-national levels, would contribute to improving aid transparency. Austria's approach to communication and development education has been reinforced with a strategy and dedicated budgets. It works with civil society actors to raise development awareness, but could do more to reach out to civil society beyond traditional Austrian actors.

Austria launched an open data portal in early 2012.[4] This portal does not yet include information on aid disbursements. A new NGO data portal where companies, NGOs and private organisations can upload data was also launched in 2013.[5] More than 1 300 datasets had been published in 2013, and close to 250 applications were based on these datasets.

Despite these commendable efforts, Austria ranked 29th out of 50 bilateral agencies in these categories.[6] One of the greatest challenges for Austria is to communicate results to major stakeholders, a step that requires an effective results-based management system (6.1.1). Achieving full compliance with the common standard by the end of 2015, and making information on all aid activities (managed by the federal government and local authorities) available through the government's open data portal, will be vital next steps. Austria is also encouraged to engage in international initiatives, such as the Open Government Partnership,[7] to share its approach to increasing transparency with the wider international community.

Domestic accountability is weak

Engaging in a public debate on development co-operation and improving domestic accountability are challenges for Austria. While the MFA shares the annual report on ODA and the triennial strategies approved by the Council of Ministers with parliament, the Sub-Committee for Development Co-operation does not scrutinise the aid programme, and discussions are mostly restricted to the budget. For its part, the Federal Ministry of Finance provides regular mid-term reports and relevant information to parliament on the occasion of the replenishment of the multilateral and regional development banks. Sensitising the various groups of parliamentarians, and ensuring that they are informed about development results achieved throughout the aid programme, could secure their more active engagement in development co-operation. The MFA may want to reflect strategically on how to achieve this.

Involvement of the NGO community, think tanks and universities in ensuring domestic accountability is also limited. The peer review team heard that these actors would like to engage in a dialogue with the Austrian federal government in a more open, structured and

sustainable way. Building on previous experiences, including with the Development Jour Fixe, would allow them to play a more active role in holding the government to account for its development commitments and results (Chapter 1). The new NGO data portal may present an opportunity for these actors to pursue government accountability and effectiveness. Interacting with government through open data projects could also help shape government data practices.

Austria performs well on sharing organisation-level information, but does not have a strategic approach to communicating results

Austrian public opinion surveys reflect a pattern common to most DAC donors: while public support for aid and development co-operation is relatively high, people know relatively little about development issues. The Eurobarometer data on Austrian attitudes reveal that the share of citizens who think helping people in developing countries is important is high (82%); the share who think the promise to increase aid to these countries should be respected is also relatively high (56%); and 18% think that aid should be increased (EC, 2013). According to a recent study by an Austrian behavioural research institute, Austrians perceive development co-operation as a positive undertaking, but are critical of the geographic spread of Austria's limited resources and would like to see more transparency and better reporting on activities and expenditures.[8]

Austria performs well on sharing organisation-level information. The ADC website is clear, complete and user friendly, and it is translated into different languages. All important messages, and policy and strategic documents are available on the website, which also includes a database of all approved projects.[9] All country offices are encouraged to communicate about their projects, using their own websites and databases. The annual reports on ODA provide some qualitative and quantitative information on results achieved by a limited number of projects with the support of the federal ministries, federal state governments, NGOs and other actors. The reports include stories about how people's lives have been improved by these projects. Having a more strategic approach to communicating about results which also addresses the issue of risks, and increasing transparency about how ADC is working and what it is achieving, would meet the concerns expressed by the Austrian public, and contribute to promoting a culture that is more open to publishing information.

The Federal Ministry of Finance communicates development results and lessons learned from its international financial institutions (IFI) programmes to selected stakeholders on an ad hoc basis (e.g. a presentation of the World Bank/Austria Urban Partnership Programme). The annual development report of the Austrian Development Bank presents the results and impacts of its programmes.

ADC has a development communication strategy; more effort is needed to reach out to civil society beyond the traditional Austrian actors

The 2009 peer review recommended that Austria "prioritise and increase resources for a comprehensive and well-targeted communication and advocacy strategy that promotes public and political debate about development in [the country]" (OECD, 2009). Austria has since published the strategy on development communication and education (ADA, 2010), as well as the guidelines for the visibility of Austrian Development Cooperation (ADA, 2012a). The strategy is flexible and supports the funding of a broad spectrum of approaches and perspectives, in terms of both content and methods. However, it does not specify how it can support the political debate on development in Austria. Interacting systematically with or supporting domestic advocacy NGOs, even if these organisations challenge the government policy on ODA, could stimulate a broad public debate on development and provide opportunities for the government to engage in political debates.

The ADA's Development Communication and Education Unit operates with a staff of three and an annual budget of EUR 4 million. Half this budget is dedicated to development education activities; the other half supports campaigns and advocacy work as well as cultural activities, publications, the media, etc.[10] The effect of the ADA's funding is perceived as positive.

A recurrent challenge, pointed out in the last peer review, is to reach out to civil society beyond the traditional Austrian NGOs. Conducting public consultations when developing the three-year programmes, engaging more strategically with the media to obtain balanced media coverage of development challenges, and integrating development education into existing teacher education programmes may be useful next steps. The ADA's Development Communication and Education Unit could also monitor the impact of communication and development education activities, e.g. by using surveys and polls to adjust the communication strategy to different audiences and evolving information needs.

Notes

1. "Evaluation of development programmes: DAC Principles for Evaluation Development", www.oecd.org/development/evaluation/dacprinciplesforevaluationdevelopmentassistance.htm.

2. OECD Development Assistance Committee (2010), DAC Guidelines and Reference Series: Quality Standards for Development Evaluation, OECD Publishing, Paris, http://dx.doi.org/10.1787/9789264083905-en.

3. As of July 2014, 11 evaluations were available on the DEReC website, covering the period May 2009-July 2014, www.oecd.org/derec/austria/publicationsdocuments/all/.

4. See more at: www.entwicklung.at/nc/zahlen-daten-und-fakten/projektliste/?tx_sysfirecdlist_pi1%5Btest%5D=test&tx_sysfirecdlist_pi1%5Bpointer%5D=24&tx_sysfirecdlist_pi1%5Bmode%5D=1&tx_sysfirecdlist_pi1%5Bsort%5D=uid%3A1.

5. ePSIplatform (2014), "Open Data by Administrations and Businesses – the Austrian Success Story", 21 July 2014, www.epsiplatform.eu/content/open-data-administrations-and-businesses-austrian-success-story#sthash.HewjT7Ob.dpuf.

6. See more at http://ati.publishwhatyoufund.org/donor/austria.

7. A new global initiative, launched in 2011, which aims to bring developed and developing country governments and civil society together in the drive towards greater openness and transparency in government. See more at: www.opengovpartnership.org/.

8. The study was conducted by Karmasin Motivforschung.
See more at: www.bmeia.gv.at/fileadmin/user_upload/bmeia/media/1-Home_Zentrale/Publikationen/Studie_Entwicklungszusammenarbeit.pdf.

9. See more at: www.entwicklung.at/zahlen-daten-und-fakten/projecktliste.

10. The unit's budget makes up approximately 45% of the overall budget of the organisations concerned. The remaining 55% is provided by contributions from third (private) parties and other public funding. According to the MFA, the 45:55 cost-sharing ratio has been stable over the years.

Bibliography

Government sources

ADA (Austrian Development Agency) (2014), *Evaluation. Austrian Partnerships Programme in Higher Education and Research for Development (APPEAR): Mid-term Evaluation. Final Report*, ADA, Vienna, www.entwicklung.at/uploads/media/APPEAR_MidtermEvaluation_Finalreport.pdf.

ADA (2013a), *Evaluation. Austrian Development Cooperation: Bhutan Country Strategy 2010-2013. Mid-term review report*, ADA, Vienna, www.entwicklung.at/uploads/media/Evaluation_Mid-Term_Review_Bhutan_Final_Report_01.pdf.

ADA (2013b), *Evaluation. Private Sector Development of the Austrian Development Cooperation. Final Report*, ADA, Vienna, www.oecd.org/derec/austria/Evaluation_private_sector_final_report_01.pdf.

ADA (2012a), *Guidelines. Visibility of Austrian Development Cooperation*, ADA, Vienna, www.entwicklung.at/uploads/media/E_Guidelines_Visibility_ADC_October_2012_05.pdf.

ADA (2012b), *Evaluation of the Austrian Development Cooperation Gender Policy between 2004-2011*. Final Report, ADA, Vienna, www.oecd.org/derec/austria/Final%20Evaluation%20Report%20GENDER.pdf.

ADA (2011), *Focus: Parliaments and Poverty Reduction*, ADA, Vienna, www.entwicklung.at/uploads/media/Focus_Parliaments_July2011_01.pdf.

ADA (2010), *Development Communication and Education in Austria. Strategy*, ADA, Vienna, www.entwicklung.at/uploads/media/Strategy_Development_Communication_April2010_02.pdf.

ADA (2008), *Leitfaden für Projekt-und Programmevaluierungen*, ADA, Vienna, www.entwicklung.at/uploads/media/leitfaden_evaluierung.pdf.

MFA (Federal Ministry for Europe, Integration and Foreign Affairs) (2014), *OECD DAC Peer Review of Austria: Memorandum*, MFA, Vienna.

Other sources

EC (European Commission) (2013), *EU Development Aid and the Millennium Development Goals, Special Eurobarometer 405,* European Commission, Brussels, http://ec.europa.eu/public_opinion/archives/ebs/ebs_405_en.pdf.

EC (2011), *Making a Difference in the World: Europeans and the Future of Development, Special Eurobarometer 375*, European Commission, Brussels, http://ec.europa.eu/public_opinion/archives/ebs/ebs_375_en.pdf.

EC (2010), Europeans, *Development Aid, and the Millennium Development Goals, Special Eurobarometer 352*, European Commission, Brussels, http://ec.europa.eu/public_opinion/archives/ebs/ebs_352_en.pdf.

EC (2009), *Development Aid in Times of Economic Turmoil, Special Eurobarometer 318*, European Commission, Brussels, http://ec.europa.eu/public_opinion/archives/ebs/ebs_318_en.pdf.

OECD (2014), *"Progress report on results measurement and management work"*, DCD/DAC(2014)5, 25 March 2014, OECD, Paris.

OECD (2010), *Evaluation in Development Agencies*, OECD Publishing, Paris, http://dx.doi.org/10.1787/9789264094857-en.

OECD (2009), *Austria: Development Assistance Committee (DAC) Peer Review,* OECD Publishing, Paris, http://dx.doi.org/10.1787/1996580x.

Chapter 7: Austria's humanitarian assistance

Strategic framework

Indicator: Clear political directives and strategies for resilience, response and recovery

Austria has a strong historical involvement with some themes of humanitarian assistance, especially human rights and the protection of civilians. It can also provide multi-annual funding to NGO partners that allows them to adapt programmes to evolving recovery contexts. There is a commitment to support the "self-help capacities" of vulnerable populations; this is mostly done through the World Bank's risk reduction facility. Austria could reflect on these achievements and develop a strategic focus for its humanitarian programme in order to increase predictability and raise its profile on the international stage. Commitments to scale up the humanitarian budget – currently suffering from very limited resources – should also be kept.

Some good thematic experience; this could provide a much needed focus for the humanitarian programme

Austria has good experience in some thematic areas of humanitarian assistance, especially protection of civilians; however, this experience has not yet been translated into a strategic focus for the humanitarian programme despite the recommendation of the 2010 *Evaluation of the Humanitarian Aid of the Austrian Development Cooperation 2004-2008* that there should be a binding humanitarian strategy with a clear objective (MFA, 2010). Austria's key humanitarian documents, including the strategic guideline on humanitarian aid (MFA, 2007) and the Austrian Security Strategy (Federal Chancellery, 2013), provide little guidance in terms of orientation or expected results from Austria's humanitarian effort. They do, however, reference the Good Humanitarian Donorship principles (GHD, 2003), which Austria has endorsed. Austria could look to build on its work promoting the protection of civilians within the United Nations Security Council,[1] and on its strong reputation in the field of human rights, to provide a thematic focus for its future humanitarian programme. This would help improve predictability for its partners and raise Austria's profile on the international stage.

No special arrangements to ensure that recovery is supported

According to the security and development strategy, humanitarian aid can "pave the way for sustainable development at an early stage" (MFA, 2011a). Austria reports that it looks for projects that include recovery and transition elements (MFA, 2014). However, there are no special tools or added flexibility to make sure these elements are included, although the ADA can provide two-year funding to NGO partners, allowing them to plan for the medium term in protracted crisis situations.

A commitment to risk reduction, delivered (mostly) through the World Bank

The strategic guideline on humanitarian aid notes that Austria should provide support to build the "self-help capacities" of affected populations and thus promote a gradual transformation away from external interventions (MFA, 2007). In practice, most of Austria's risk reduction programming is executed through the Federal Ministry of Finance, which has funded the World Bank's disaster risk reduction facility[2] since 2012. There are also good interactions with the World Bank's regional disaster risk management team, based in Vienna. Other NGO and UN partners report that funding for risk reduction and resilience programming is not readily available.

Funding levels do not match Austria's humanitarian ambitions

Austria allocated 3.3% of its total ODA to its own humanitarian assistance programme in 2012, a smaller share than would be expected from a DAC member.[3] This is down from a peak of 7% in 2009, during Austria's Security Council membership. While the total amount of Austria's humanitarian assistance in 2012 was EUR 40.4 million (or approximately USD 51.9 million), nearly 60% is provided through assessed contributions to the EU (MFA, 2014), leaving Austria with only USD 18.1 million[4] for its own humanitarian efforts. As pointed out by the 2010 evaluation, these limited financial resources do not allow Austria to play a "distinctive role" (MFA, 2010). If Austria wishes to be a Good Humanitarian Donor, it will need to raise these levels. It has made a political commitment to allocate EUR 20 million per year to the Federal Disaster Response Fund (MFA, 2014), compared to the current EUR 5 million; however, this has not yet become reality despite broad cross-party support.[5]

Effective programme design

Indicator: Programmes target the highest risk to life and livelihood

Austria needs to develop clear funding allocation criteria, applicable across government and based on its comparative advantage, if it is to deliver consistent and measurable results from its fragmented programme, increase predictability for partners, and guard against the risk of politicisation of the aid programme.

Clearer, cross-government allocation criteria would increase predictability, reduce fragmentation and guard against politicisation

The 2010 evaluation of humanitarian aid called for clear criteria for funding allocations in order to increase the transparency of decision-making and counter fragmentation across government (MFA, 2010); this recommendation remains pertinent. Current procedures have resulted in a highly fragmented programme, with 76 different countries and regions funded in 2012 (Figure 7.1).

By law, funding from the Foreign Disaster Relief Fund is to be determined by the Council of Ministers, potentially a risk to the apolitical and principled nature of humanitarian assistance, as well as usually a rather slow process in practice. Information gathered from Austria's presence in crisis countries is combined with EU information products and humanitarian appeals to inform proposals to Ministers, but this is a very ad-hoc process. Partners are chosen for their reliability, and there is a focus on multilateral partners (Figure 7.1) but no clear strategy to support these allocations. NGO partners who are accredited by the EU are automatically eligible for Austrian funding; ADA will also vet and approve other NGOs. The overall decision-making process could therefore be tightened.

The Federal Ministry of the Interior, which supports civil protection deployments, has its own decision-making process based on international information sources, with the ultimate decision to deploy coming from its director. Funding for food aid, through the Federal Ministry of Agriculture, Forestry, Environment and Water Management, is based on discussions with the World Food Programme (WFP) and the Food and Agriculture Organization (FAO), as well as in consultation with the ADA and the MFA.

Clearer allocation criteria, applicable across government and based on Austria's comparative advantage, would help Austria deliver more consistent and measurable results from its cross-government humanitarian programme, increase predictability for partners, and guard against the risk of politicisation of the aid programme.

Early warning is not a major focus

As in the case of many other donors, there is no clear link between early warning and early response.

Participation through partner programmes

Austria requires its NGO partners to support active participation by affected populations throughout the programme cycle; this is a pre-requisite for funding. Given Austria's limited humanitarian presence in crisis areas, this is the most practical approach to ensuring participation.

Box 7.1 Austria's funding allocations, 2012

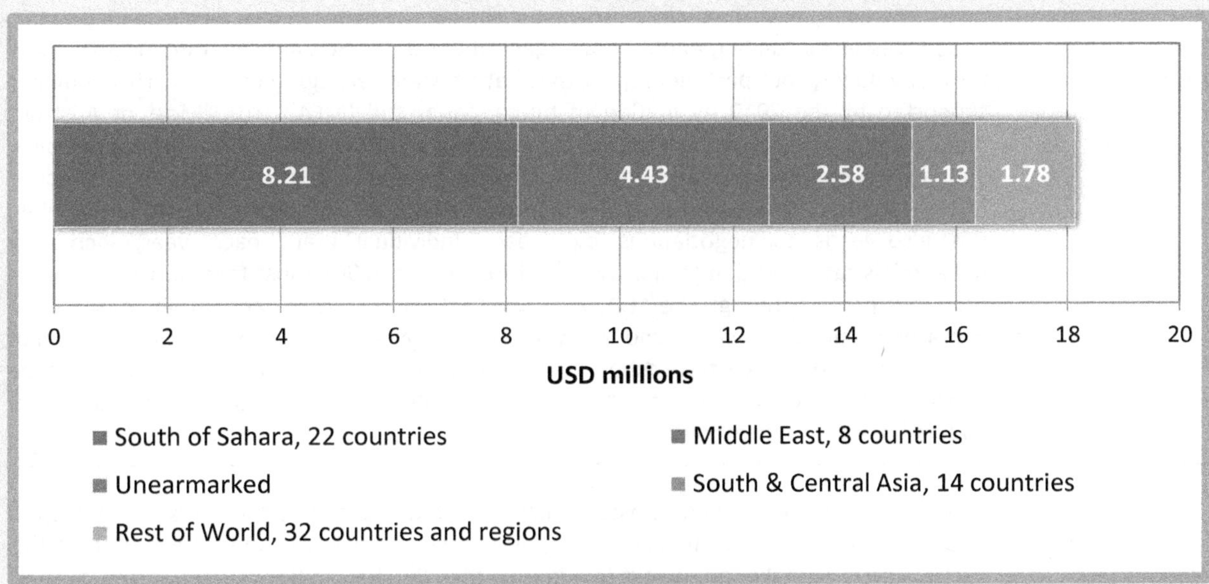

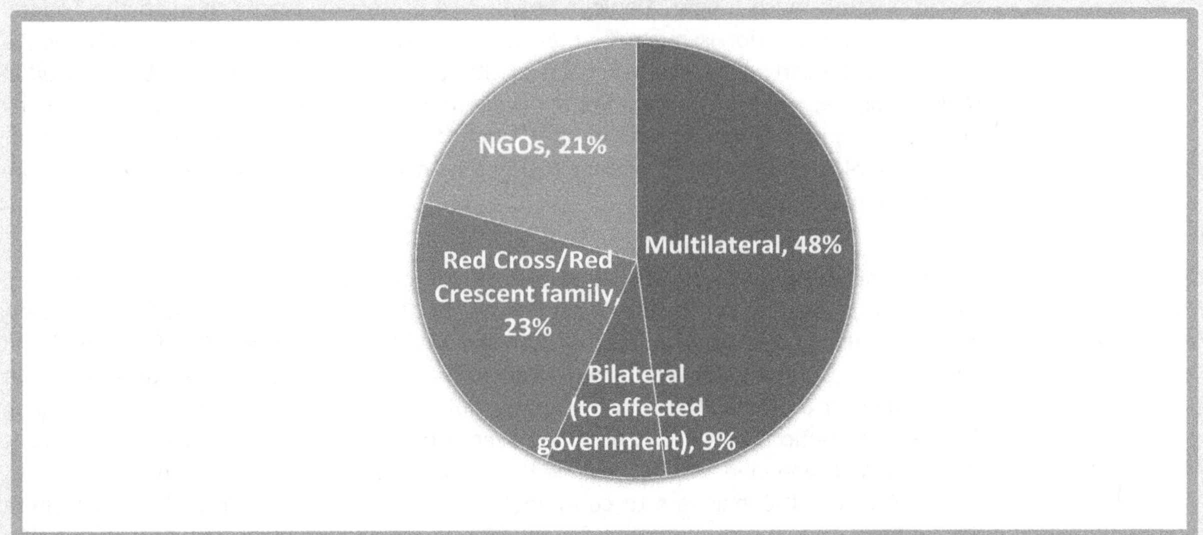

Source: OECD Creditor Reporting System. Gross disbursements in current prices.

Effective delivery, partnerships and instruments

Indicator: Delivery modalities and partnerships help deliver quality assistance

Austria's funding to multilateral agencies is only lightly earmarked; this is good practice. However, allocations fluctuate significantly and must be renegotiated each year, hampering predictability. Many grants and bilateral interventions are very small. They could be scaled up or consolidated to increase efficiency. The timeliness of disbursements for new and escalating crises is also an issue; here Austria relies on its civil protection deployments, which are much quicker than funding to partners. Addressing all these issues contributes to a high administrative burden for Austria's partners.

Tools for protracted crises are not predictable

The processes for funding multilateral organisations and NGOs are separate, as is the case for many donors, but partners report that both systems are quite complex. This finding is supported by the 2010 evaluation of humanitarian aid (MFA, 2010). Most of Austria's multilateral funding is earmarked, but often only to the crisis level; this improves flexibility and is good practice. However, the lack of clear criteria (7.2.1) and a strategic objective (7.1.1) for the humanitarian programme means Austria's allocations are not predictable; this also leads to negotiations over each individual grant each year, increasing the administrative burden for partners and for Austria. NGOs must take part in a call-for-proposals process through the ADA, with two to three such calls per year. Funding can be allocated for up to two years, and the ADA reports that grants should be for a minimum of EUR 200 000, to reduce transaction costs; this is a useful approach that could also be applied across government – in 2012, 137 of Austria's funding allocations (out of a total of 162) fell below this threshold.[6]

Timeliness can be an issue in rapid response situations

Allocations from the Foreign Disaster Relief Fund, once agreed by Ministers, are passed to the ADA, which initiates the call-for-proposals process for NGOs and others. At best this decision cycle can take four weeks (e.g. during the 2014 Balkan floods), but partners report that it is often much longer. Deployment of civil protection teams through the Federal Ministry of the Interior is much quicker, and the Austrian system relies on this tool to respond in the early days of a new disaster situation. The military can also be involved in rapid response, mostly by facilitating co-ordination in countries where they are already present, for example as peacekeepers (Chapter 5). Hence, Austria should perhaps limit itself to civil protection and military responses to rapid onset crises and refrain from making grants.

Slow decision-making and lack of predictability increase partners' administrative burden

Funding provided to most UN partners is either core or only lightly earmarked (MFA, 2014), meeting the recommendation of the 2009 review (OECD, 2009). However, decision-making takes time (funds are often received towards the middle of the year) and amounts fluctuate significantly from year to year, meaning Austria's funding is not predictable for partners. The Ministry responsible for food aid is an exception, providing flexible contributions (which can be rolled over at the year's end) in two tranches – one at the beginning and one at the end of the year. Unusually for a humanitarian donor, Austria likes its NGO partners to co-finance humanitarian interventions; however, there are no fixed rules and it sometimes funds 100% of programme costs. Dialogue with NGOs has increased through the new Humanitarian Platform, but this is mostly an information-sharing forum. It would be useful to enlarge the scope of the Humanitarian Platform to include strategy and results.

Austria co-ordinates with other donors

Austria is a member of all the usual donor groups (MFA, 2014).[7] It also collaborates closely with Norway on issues related to human rights and the protection of civilians. As Austria is not often present in the field, most of this co-ordination occurs at capital level.

Organisation fit for purpose

Indicator: Systems, structures, processes and people work together effectively and efficiently

There is significant fragmentation in Austria's humanitarian system; this limits Austria's ability to make the most of its humanitarian resources and expertise. Civil-military co-ordination is a focus for Austria, including training its own (and ECOWAS) peacekeeping troops in an effort to enlarge its humanitarian space. Partners report good relationships with Austrian humanitarian staff.

Efforts to strengthen cross-government co-ordination could help reduce fragmentation

The 2009 peer review flagged both the fragmentation of humanitarian aid across government, and the informal, personality-based co-ordination system, as serious issues (OECD, 2009); this finding was echoed by the evaluation of humanitarian aid (MFA, 2010) and remains a concern today. The strategic guideline on humanitarian aid outlined the roles of different actors in the system (MFA, 2007). This structure remains unchanged, although Austria notes that the MFA is now the lead entity, hosting regular co-ordination meetings (MFA, 2014). Reflection on cross-government co-ordination is encouraged, so that Austria can make the most of its humanitarian resources and expertise to forge more effective humanitarian results.

Support to civil-military co-ordination

Austria deploys its military for disaster response, mostly using its logistics and engineering skills and assets (MFA, 2014). The strategic guideline recognises the need to comply with international guidance on military deployment (IASC, 2008; OCHA, 2007). Although there are no active safeguards in place, no issues were raised during this peer review period. Austria also helps support civil-military co-ordination, especially in the Balkans, and supports civil-military training of ECOWAS soldiers before their deployment on peacekeeping missions.[8] It provides similar training to Austrian soldiers awaiting peacekeeping duties (Chapter 5).

Good relationships between partners and staff

Partners report good, open relationships with Austria's humanitarian staff across government. The evaluation noted that there were sufficient staff in the system to cope with a scale-up in humanitarian assistance, but did recommend rebalancing to increase ADA staff and decrease MFA headcount (MFA, 2010), although Austria reports that there is no scope for this occurring in practice. It is beyond the scope of this review to determine where staff should be posted, but this issue could be taken into account as Austria discusses its strategic orientation for humanitarian assistance and looks at ways to reduce institutional fragmentation.

Results, learning and accountability

Indicator: Results are measured and communicated, and lessons learnt

The evaluation of humanitarian aid in 2010 was useful, but very few of its recommendations have been implemented. Monitoring of Austria's on-going performance as a humanitarian donor is complicated, as it has not yet set out verifiable indicators for the cross-government programme. Partner activities and results are monitored, mostly through reports, dialogue and field visits, but this is difficult when Austria provides funding for so many different crises. Information about the humanitarian programme is made public.

Useful evaluation recommendations were not implemented; setting targets to monitor could be useful

Austria conducted a thorough evaluation of its humanitarian aid covering the years 2004-08, comparing itself to Germany, Norway, the Netherlands and Switzerland (MFA, 2010). However, very few of the recommendations have been implemented. The management response indicated that Austria would be unable to implement most of the recommendations due to the lack of volume and predictability of its humanitarian assistance (MFA, 2011b); this is surprising given that recommendations to develop a strategic approach and reduce fragmentation, and to improve funding criteria and monitoring do not necessarily require volume or predictability (although that would, admittedly, make the job easier). Austria does not have an easy task in monitoring its performance as a humanitarian donor, given that it has not set any targets. It did not respond to the Good Humanitarian Donorship's monitoring of indicators in 2013. As Austria moves to establish a strategic direction for its humanitarian programme, it could identify verifiable indicators that would help monitor its performance.

Monitoring of partners continues

The 2009 peer review recommended that Austria strengthen its humanitarian evaluation and learning (OECD, 2009). The peer team heard that the ADA has strict controls on value for money in its NGO programme; other parts of government note that partner results (often multilateral agencies) are monitored through annual financial and narrative reports, dialogue and field visits (MFA, 2014). Partners are encouraged to integrate review and evaluation elements into their programmes, as there is no independent monitoring budget. It is not clear how results and lessons are documented or shared. Decreasing fragmentation of the programme (7.2.1) would help Austria focus its monitoring efforts.

Existing information is made public

The annual ODA reports include information on the humanitarian programme, including significant grants and information on particular projects. Further details and policy documents are available in English and German on the ADC website.[9]

Notes

1. During Austria's two-year Security Council membership (2009-10), it oversaw the unanimous adoption in 2009 of resolution 1894 on the protection of civilians in armed conflict.

2. The Global Facility for Disaster Reduction and Recovery (GFDRR) (www.gfdrr.org).

3. On average, OECD/DAC members allocated 8.9% of their ODA to humanitarian assistance in 2012. Allocations ranged from 0.1% to 16.6%. In 2012 Austria allocated USD 18.14 million (gross disbursements in current prices) to humanitarian assistance, equivalent to 3.3% of total ODA that year. Source: OECD Creditor Reporting System.

4. Figures are gross disbursements in current prices. Source: OECD Creditor Reporting System.

5. The Austrian Red Cross report that 107 of 183 members of parliament, from all political groups, were in favour of withdrawing the cuts to the Federal Disaster Response Fund. More (in German) at www.roteskreuz.at/organisieren/gesellschaftspolitik/governmentwatchat/nicht-umgesetzt/internationale-solidaritaet-entwicklung-und-humanitaere-hilfe/?sword_list[]=auslandskatastrophenfonds&no_cache=1.

6. Figures are gross disbursements in current prices. Source: OECD Creditor Reporting System.

7. Austria is a member of the Good Humanitarian Donorship initiative, the United Nations Office for the Coordination of Humanitarian Affairs (OCHA) Donor Support Group, and the European Council's Working Group on Humanitarian Aid and Food Aid (COHAFA).

8. Austria's Ministry of Defence supplies the course director for the Kofi Annan International Peacekeeping Training Centre's civil-military training programme (www.kaiptc.org).

9. Austrian Development Cooperation, "Humanitarian Aid", www.entwicklung.at/en/funding/humanitarian-aid/.

Bibliography

Government sources

Federal Chancellery (2013), *Austrian Security Strategy: Security in a New Decade – Shaping Security*, Federal Chancellery of the Republic of Austria, Vienna, www.bka.gv.at/DocView.axd?CobId=52251.

MFA (Federal Ministry for Europe, Integration and Foreign Affairs) (2014), *OECD DAC Peer review of Austria: Memorandum*, April 2014, MFA, Vienna.

MFA (2011a), *Security and Development in Austrian Development Policy – Strategic Guideline,* MFA, Vienna, www.entwicklung.at/uploads/media/StratGuide_Security_and_Development.pdf.

MFA (2011b), *Management Response – Humanitäre Hilfe Der Oeza (2004-2008) – Entwurf 15.3.2011,* unpublished.

MFA (2010), *Evaluation of the Humanitarian Aid of the Austrian Development Cooperation 2004-2008*, MFA, Vienna, www.entwicklung.at/uploads/media/Executive_summary.pdf.

MFA (2007), *Strategic Guideline on International Humanitarian Aid of the Austrian Development Cooperation*, MFA, Vienna.

Other sources

GHD (Good Humanitarian Donorship) (2003), "Principles and Good Practice of Humanitarian Donorship" (endorsed in Stockholm, Sweden, 17 June 2003), http://reliefweb.int/report/world/principles-and-good-practice-humanitarian-donorship.

IASC (Inter-Agency Standing Committee) (2008), *Civil-Military Guidelines and Reference for Complex Emergencies* (comprising: Civil-Military Relationship in Complex Emergencies – an IASC Reference Paper [June 2004]; Guidelines on the Use of Military and Civil Defence Assets to Support United Nations Humanitarian Activities in Complex Emergencies – "MCDA Guidelines" – Rev. 1 [January 2006]; Use of Military or Armed Escorts for Humanitarian Convoys – IASC Discussion Paper and Non-Binding Guidelines [September 2001]; and Annexes and References), IASC with OCHA, Geneva, www.refworld.org/pdfid/47da82a72.pdf.

OCHA (United Nations Office for the Co-ordination of Humanitarian Affairs) (2007), *Guidelines on the Use of Foreign Military and Civil Defence Assets in Disaster Relief* – "Oslo Guidelines" – Rev. 1.1, OCHA, Geneva, http://vosocc.unocha.org/Documents/29786_OSLO%20Guidelines%20Rev%201.pdf.

OECD (2009), *Austria: Development Assistance Committee (DAC) Peer Review*, OECD Publishing, Paris, http://dx.doi.org/10.1787/1996580x.

Annex A: Progress since the 2009 DAC Peer Review recommendations

Key Issues: Towards a comprehensive development effort

Recommendations 2009	Progress in implementation
Deepen commitment to and move forward on policy coherence for development. Austria needs to publish clearly-prioritised and time-bound action agendas; to clarify mandates and responsibilities for policy coherence for development; and to build a system for analysis, monitoring and reporting which includes perspectives and experiences from the field. Austria should look to the experiences of other DAC members.	**Partially implemented**

Key Issues: Policy vision and strategic orientations

Recommendations 2009	Progress in implementation
Prepare a medium-term development policy such as a "white paper", which addresses all ODA activities and is endorsed at the political level. This should commit all Austrian aid at the strategic level to the primary objectives of Austrian development co-operation, including Austria's commitment to implementing the Paris Declaration principles. Such a medium-term development policy, prepared under the leadership of the MFA, could be an effective instrument for increasing coherence in Austria's aid system and bringing all aid-spending ministries in line with, and accountable to, the objectives of the Development Co-operation Act.	**Partially implemented**

Key Issues: ODA allocations

Recommendations 2009	Progress in implementation
Continue to make progress towards meeting the ODA/GNI target of 0.7% in 2015. Reaching its interim target of 0.51% in 2010 is essential even in an environment of financial crisis. This would send a strong, positive signal to the development community.	**Not implemented**

Develop a specific plan containing annual targets for reaching these commitments. This is necessary to give credibility to Austria's aid promises and will make aid volumes more predictable for partner countries and other development partners. Any increase in Austrian aid should prioritise existing country and multilateral programmes. Austria should not rely on debt relief as a significant component for meeting its ODA commitments.	**Not implemented**
Implement Paris Club debt relief decisions without delay to ensure that recipients receive the benefit of relief promptly, and that Austria's ODA figures are fully comparable with those of other donors. It is important for the Ministry of Finance to communicate Paris Club decisions in a timely manner to the MFA.	**Partially implemented**

Key Issues: Organisation fit for purpose

Recommendations 2009	Progress in implementation
Fine-tune the organisation of Austria's aid system to deal with capacity pressures and to clarify roles and responsibilities between the MFA and ADA. Austria should ensure that the MFA has the required resources to meet its responsibilities to set policy, give strategic direction, monitor and evaluate, and report on results.	**Partially implemented**

Key Issues: Delivery modalities and partnerships for quality aid

Recommendations 2009	Progress in implementation
Concentrate the aid programme to improve efficiency and effectiveness, as previously recommended in the 2004 DAC peer review. Austria should set up efforts to diminish the fragmentation of total ODA and of the aid programme managed by ADA. The MFA should use *ex ante* aid allocations by all ministries to help achieve greater coherence in the aid policy, and build the transparency and predictability of total ODA.	**Partially implemented**

Provide co-financing for multi-annual result-oriented programmes of NGOs with sufficient demonstrated capacity in programme management. This will help reduce transaction costs and give NGOs more flexibility and predictability.	**Partially implemented**
Complement the Aid Effectiveness Action Plan with a binding, system-wide operational plan for taking forward the lessons from Austria's aid effectiveness review. These include increasing the emphasis on results; clarifying the division of labour between ADA and the MFA in their relations with the field; making aid more predictable; using partners' monitoring, evaluation and reporting procedures and systems; and identifying appropriate niche sectors as it improves division of labour and increases country programmable aid.	**Partially implemented**

Key Issues: Results, transparency and accountability

Recommendations 2009	Progress in implementation
Strengthen efforts to win political and public support for development co-operation, in particular for achieving international aid targets and the MDGs. The MFA should take the lead on developing, in consultation with the MoF, ADA and other government stakeholders, a comprehensive and well-targeted communication and advocacy strategy that promotes public and political debate about development in Austria. Austria is encouraged to build on its good practice in global education and share this experience with other donors.	**Partially implemented**
Develop a culture of managing for results in Austria's aid system by placing results at the centre of planning, implementation, disbursement reporting, monitoring and evaluation and staff performance objectives. Country programmes should have specific results frameworks, which should align with partner countries' own objectives.	**Partially implemented**
Bring Austria's evaluation system in line with DAC guidelines on evaluation. An independent evaluation unit with sufficient staff and budget needs to be established within the MFA.	**Implemented**

Key Issues: Humanitarian assistance

Recommendations 2009	Progress in implementation
Bolster support to UN agencies and Red Cross organisations with un-earmarked core funding, as recommended in the Good Humanitarian Donorship Initiative, and in line with its position within the international community, as well as to establish an annual budget allocation for the Foreign Disaster Relief Fund. The recent pledge to increase significantly Austrian humanitarian assistance is very encouraging.	**Partially implemented**
Consider more streamlined approaches for support channelled through multilateral partners, including (but not limited to) multi-annual framework agreements. As the budget increases, efficiency dividends could also be gained by establishing humanitarian partnership agreements with accredited NGOs, such as those that already exist in the development sector.	**Not implemented**
Strengthen evaluation and learning functions within the humanitarian sector in line with the greater scrutiny likely to emanate from increased financial flows to the sector.	**Partially implemented**

Figure A.1 Austria's implementation of 2009 peer review recommendations

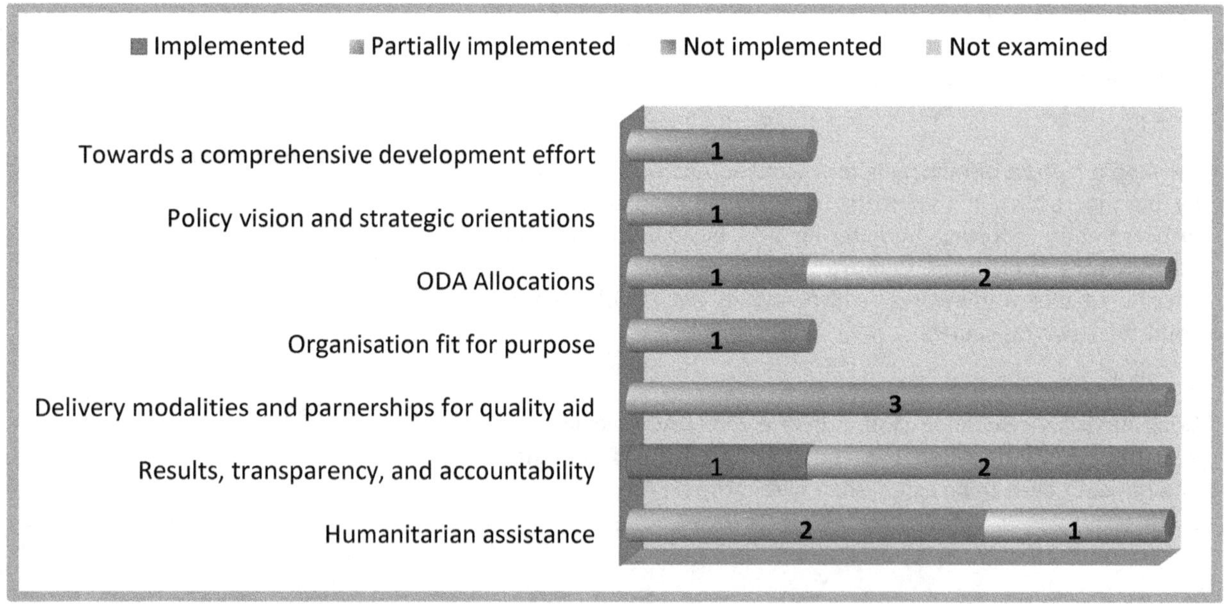

Annex B: OECD/DAC standard suite of tables

Table B.1 Total financial flows

USD million at current prices and exchange rates

Austria	1998-2002	2003-2007	2008	2009	2010	2011	2012
					Net disbursements		
Total official flows	545	1 023	1 816	1 098	1 054	1 142	1 154
Official development assistance	509	1 213	1 714	1 142	1 208	1 111	1 106
Bilateral	337	846	1 234	507	612	490	536
Multilateral	172	367	480	635	596	621	570
Other official flows	36	- 189	103	- 44	- 154	30	48
Bilateral	36	- 189	103	- 44	- 154	30	48
Multilateral	-	-	-	-	-	-	-
Net Private Grants	61	108	137	140	167	182	- 0
Private flows at market terms	770	5 167	8 878	2 035	5 150	6 751	3 380
Bilateral: *of which*	770	5 167	8 878	2 035	5 150	6 751	3 380
Direct investment	564	4 381	7 061	2 551	5 664	7 148	3 743
Export credits	206	786	1 817	- 562	- 555	- 500	- 469
Multilateral	-	-	-	-	-	-	-
Total flows	1 375	6 299	10 831	3 273	6 372	8 075	4 534
for reference:							
ODA (at constant 2011 USD million)	*815*	*1 375*	*1 633*	*1 113*	*1 218*	*1 046*	*1 106*
ODA (as a % of GNI)	*0.26*	*0.40*	*0.43*	*0.30*	*0.32*	*0.27*	*0.28*
Total flows (as a % of GNI) (a)	*0.69*	*2.06*	*2.71*	*0.87*	*1.70*	*1.94*	*1.15*
ODA to and channelled through NGOs							
- In USD million	46	59	62	90	71	64	45
- In percentage of total net ODA	9	5	4	8	6	6	4
- DAC countries' average % of total net ODA	*8*	*8*	*7*	*8*	*9*	*13*	*13*

a. To countries eligible for ODA.

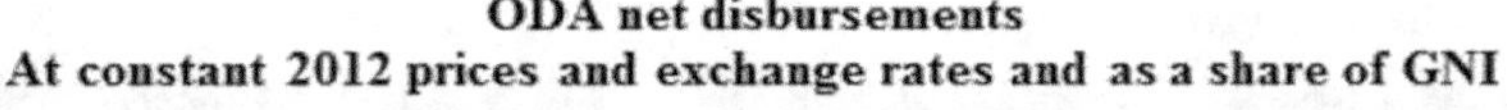

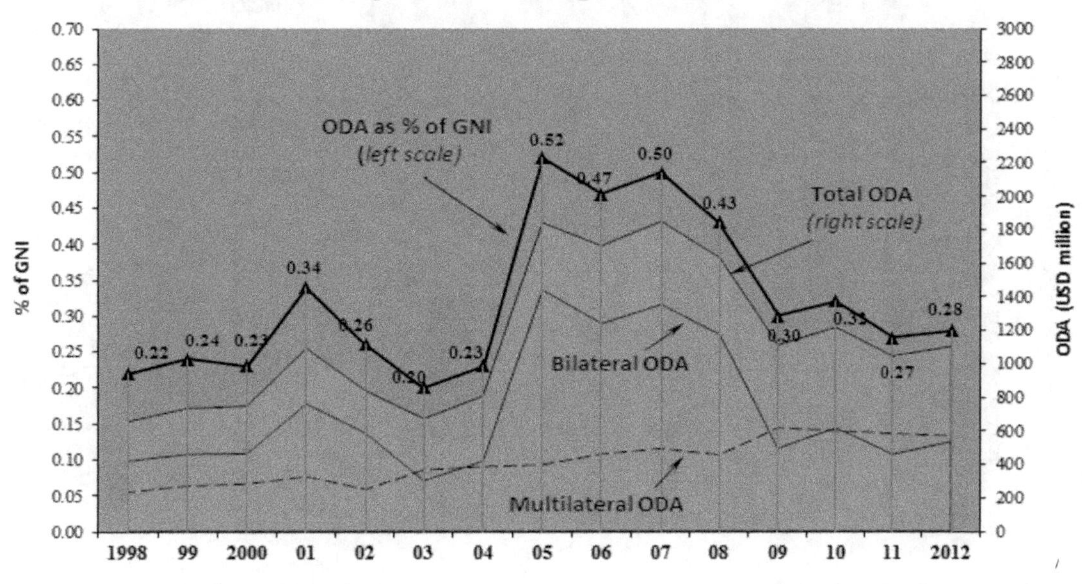

Table B.2 ODA by main categories

Disbursements

Austria	Constant 2012 USD million					Per cent share of gross disbursements					Total DAC
	2008	2009	2010	2011	2012	2008	2009	2010	2011	2012	2012%
Gross Bilateral ODA	**1 223**	**507**	**622**	**465**	**543**	**73**	**45**	**51**	**44**	**49**	**73**
General budget support	4	2	4	4	3	0	0	0	0	0	1
Core support to national NGOs	1	1	0	1	0	0	0	0	0	0	1
Investment projects	41	29	10	13	19	2	3	1	1	2	11
Debt relief grants	739	57	156	41	106	44	5	13	4	9	2
Administrative costs	38	39	38	35	33	2	3	3	3	3	5
Other in-donor expenditures	52	49	46	48	65	3	4	4	5	6	3
Gross Multilateral ODA	**457**	**619**	**602**	**585**	**570**	**27**	**55**	**49**	**56**	**51**	**27**
UN agencies	40	35	53	31	23	2	3	4	3	2	5
EU institutions	279	319	327	296	275	17	28	27	28	25	9
World Bank group	116	155	152	156	181	7	14	12	15	16	6
Regional development banks	8	100	58	68	72	0	9	5	6	6	3
Other multilateral	13	11	12	34	19	1	1	1	3	2	5
Total gross ODA	**1 680**	**1 126**	**1 224**	**1 050**	**1 113**	**100**	**100**	**100**	**100**	**100**	**100**
Repayments and debt cancellation	**- 47**	**- 13**	**- 6**	**- 4**	**- 8**						
Total net ODA	**1 633**	**1 113**	**1 218**	**1 046**	**1 106**						
For reference:											
Free standing technical co-operation	*201*	*196*	*214*	*203*	*198*						
Net debt relief	*699*	*57*	*156*	*41*	*106*						
Imputed student cost	*91*	*86*	*89*	*87*	*114*						
Refugees in donor countries	*43*	*40*	*36*	*40*	*58*						

Contributions to UN Agencies (2011-12 Average)

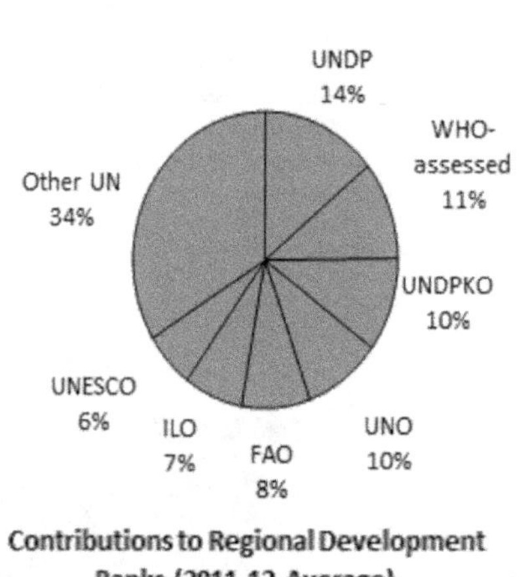

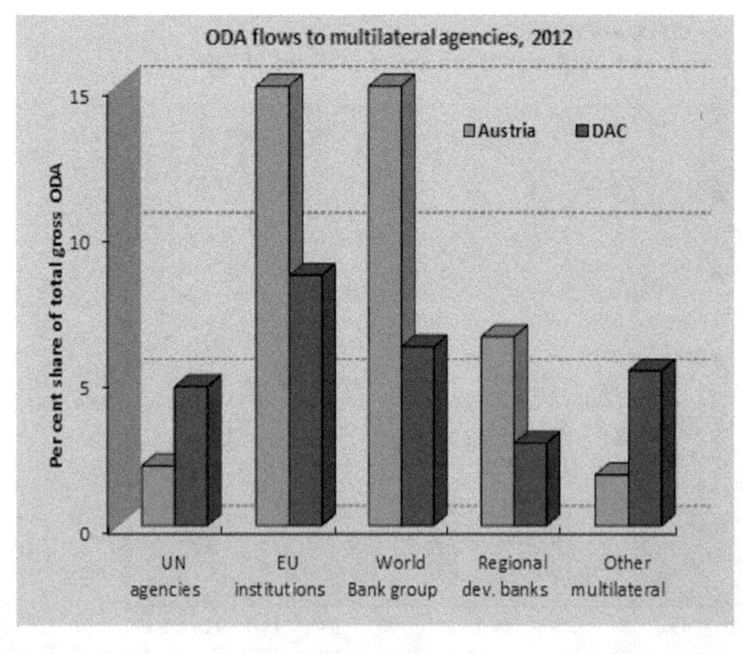

Contributions to Regional Development Banks (2011-12 Average)

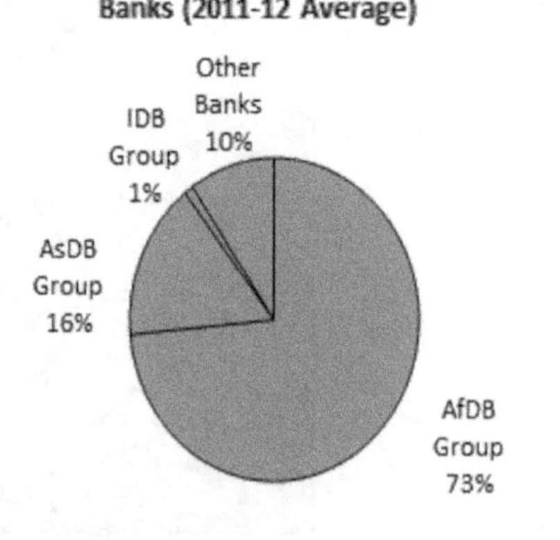

Table B.3 Bilateral ODA allocable by region and income group

Gross disbursements

Austria	Constant 2012 USD million					Per cent share					Total DAC
	2008	2009	2010	2011	2012	2008	2009	2010	2011	2012	2012%
Africa	195	147	239	120	176	18	38	47	35	43	43
Sub-Saharan Africa	163	132	221	104	166	15	34	44	31	41	37
North Africa	29	13	9	11	8	3	3	2	3	2	4
Asia	66	49	59	65	56	6	13	12	19	14	34
South and Central Asia	32	27	33	29	23	3	7	7	9	6	20
Far East	34	22	25	32	29	3	6	5	9	7	14
America	26	28	39	29	27	2	7	8	9	6	10
North and Central America	21	21	31	23	18	2	5	6	7	4	4
South America	6	5	5	5	5	1	1	1	1	1	5
Middle East	661	15	12	13	19	60	4	2	4	5	7
Oceania	1	1	1	1	1	0	0	0	0	0	2
Europe	156	144	156	113	131	14	37	31	33	32	3
Total bilateral allocable by region	1 104	384	505	341	409	100	100	100	100	100	100
Least developed	133	105	208	90	57	13	31	48	30	15	41
Other low-income	18	5	3	4	2	2	1	1	1	1	4
Lower middle-income	747	110	93	86	182	71	33	21	29	49	36
Upper middle-income	148	112	126	116	131	14	33	29	39	35	18
More advanced developing countries	9	5	6	-	-	1	2	1	-	-	-
Total bilateral allocable by income	1 054	337	435	296	373	100	100	100	100	100	100
For reference:											
Total bilateral	1 219	504	622	465	543	*100*	*100*	*100*	*100*	*100*	*100*
of which: Unallocated by region	*115*	*120*	*116*	*124*	*134*	*9*	*24*	*19*	*27*	*25*	*24*
of which: Unallocated by income	*165*	*167*	*187*	*169*	*171*	*14*	*33*	*30*	*36*	*31*	*32*

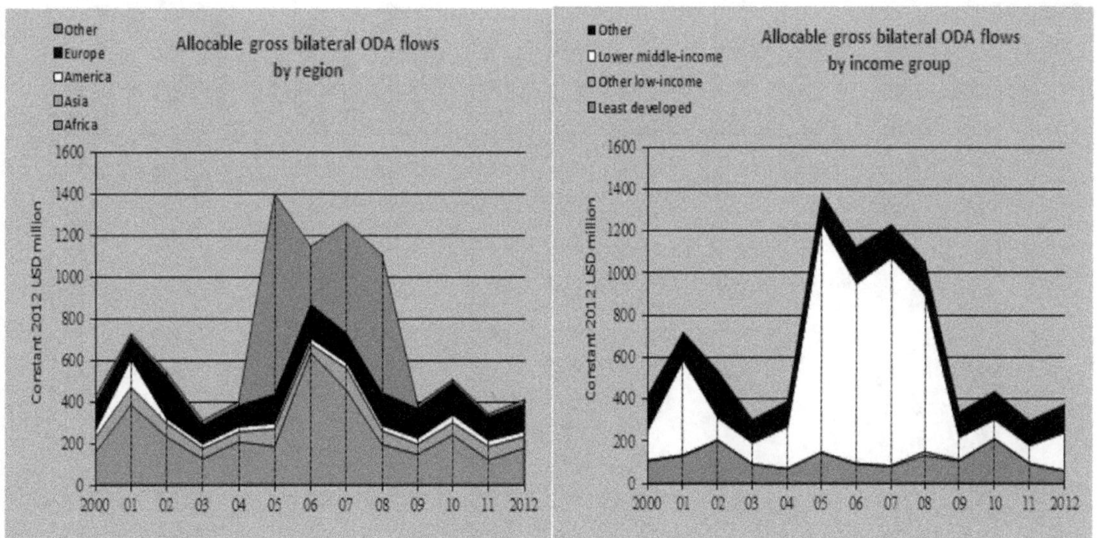

1. Each region includes regional amounts which cannot be allocated by sub-region. The sum of the sub-regional amounts may therefore fall short of the regional total.

Table B.4 Main recipients of bilateral ODA

Gross disbursements

Austria	2001-05 average			Memo:
	Current USD million	Constant 2012 USD mln	Per cent share	*DAC countries' average %*
Iraq	165	193	30	
Cameroon	44	67	8	
Serbia	38	55	7	
Egypt	20	28	4	
Turkey	17	24	3	
Top 5 recipients	**283**	**367**	**52**	**42**
Bosnia-Herzegovina	17	23	3	
Madagascar	14	18	3	
Bolivia	13	22	2	
Afghanistan	9	13	2	
Tanzania	9	14	2	
Top 10 recipients	**345**	**458**	**64**	**56**
Uganda	7	10	1	
Mozambique	7	11	1	
Nicaragua	7	10	1	
Ethiopia	6	9	1	
China	6	8	1	
Top 15 recipients	**379**	**504**	**70**	**62**
Ghana	6	7	1	
Guatemala	5	7	1	
Nigeria	5	6	1	
Iran	5	6	1	
Burkina Faso	5	6	1	
Top 20 recipients	**404**	**538**	**74**	**67**
Total (122 recipients)	496	665	91	
Unallocated	47	64	9	17
Total bilateral gross	**543**	**729**	**100**	**100**

	2006-10 average			Memo:
	Current USD million	Constant 2012 USD mln	Per cent share	*DAC countries' average %*
Iraq	283	286	29	
Cameroon	89	101	9	
Nigeria	65	66	7	
Bosnia-Herzegovina	32	33	3	
Congo, Dem. Rep.	30	30	3	
Top 5 recipients	**499**	**516**	**51**	**37**
Serbia	29	30	3	
Turkey	26	26	3	
Egypt	19	19	2	
China	16	16	2	
Ethiopia	14	14	1	
Top 10 recipients	**602**	**621**	**62**	**50**
Uganda	13	13	1	
Georgia	12	12	1	
Chad	10	10	1	
Nicaragua	8	9	1	
Mozambique	8	8	1	
Top 15 recipients	**654**	**673**	**67**	**59**
Albania	8	8	1	
Kosovo	8	8	1	
Cote d'Ivoire	7	7	1	
Croatia	7	7	1	
Ukraine	7	7	1	
Top 20 recipients	**690**	**710**	**71**	**64**
Total (131 recipients)	818	839	84	
Unallocated	157	159	16	25
Total bilateral gross	**975**	**998**	**100**	**100**

	2011-12 average			Memo:
	Current USD million	Constant 2012 USD mln	Per cent share	*DAC countries' average %*
Cote d'Ivoire	50	50	10	
Turkey	36	35	7	
Bosnia-Herzegovina	27	27	5	
China	19	18	4	
Togo	16	15	3	
Top 5 recipients	**148**	**144**	**28**	**32**
Ukraine	12	12	2	
Uganda	12	12	2	
Kosovo	12	12	2	
Serbia	11	11	2	
Ethiopia	10	10	2	
Top 10 recipients	**205**	**200**	**40**	**47**
Mozambique	10	9	2	
Albania	9	8	2	
Egypt	8	8	2	
Iran	7	7	1	
Nicaragua	7	7	1	
Top 15 recipients	**246**	**239**	**47**	**56**
Burkina Faso	7	7	1	
Vietnam	7	6	1	
Guatemala	6	6	1	
West Bank & Gaza Strip	5	5	1	
Ghana	4	4	1	
Top 20 recipients	**275**	**267**	**53**	**60**
Total (120 recipients)	344	335	66	
Unallocated	175	169	34	29
Total bilateral gross	**519**	**504**	**100**	**100**

Table B.5 Bilateral ODA by major purposes

at constant prices and exchange rates

Commitments - Two-year average

Austria	2001-2005 average		2006-10 average		2011-12 average		2011-12
	2012 USD million	Per cent	2012 USD million	Per cent	2012 USD million	Per cent	Total DAC per cent
Social infrastructure & services	207	29	270	27	339	57	41
Education	104	15	138	14	160	27	8
of which: basic education	3	0	4	0	1	0	2
Health	19	3	35	4	84	14	5
of which: basic health	14	2	10	1	3	1	4
Population & reproductive health	1	0	3	0	1	0	7
Water supply & sanitation	21	3	25	2	34	6	5
Government & civil society	53	8	59	6	49	8	13
of which: Conflict, peace & security	5	1	20	2	10	2	2
Other social infrastructure & services	9	1	10	1	11	2	2
Economic infrastructure & services	23	3	45	5	50	8	16
Transport & storage	9	1	11	1	15	3	7
Communications	3	0	0	0	-	-	0
Energy	8	1	11	1	14	2	6
Banking & financial services	1	0	8	1	6	1	2
Business & other services	1	0	13	1	15	3	1
Production sectors	20	3	24	2	19	3	8
Agriculture, forestry & fishing	8	1	12	1	14	2	5
Industry, mining & construction	9	1	6	1	5	1	2
Trade & tourism	3	0	5	1	1	0	1
Multisector	21	3	30	3	20	3	10
Commodity and programme aid	3	0	4	0	4	1	3
Action relating to debt	331	47	511	52	65	11	3
Humanitarian aid	13	2	26	3	17	3	8
Administrative costs of donors	33	5	38	4	33	6	6
Refugees in donor countries	52	7	43	4	49	8	4
Total bilateral allocable	702	100	989	100	596	100	100
For reference:							
Total bilateral	*723*	*66*	*1 003*	*64*	*607*	*54*	*74*
of which: Unallocated	*21*	*2*	*14*	*1*	*11*	*1*	*1*
Total multilateral	*370*	*34*	*564*	*36*	*514*	*46*	*26*
Total ODA	***1 094***	***100***	***1 567***	***100***	***1 121***	***100***	***100***

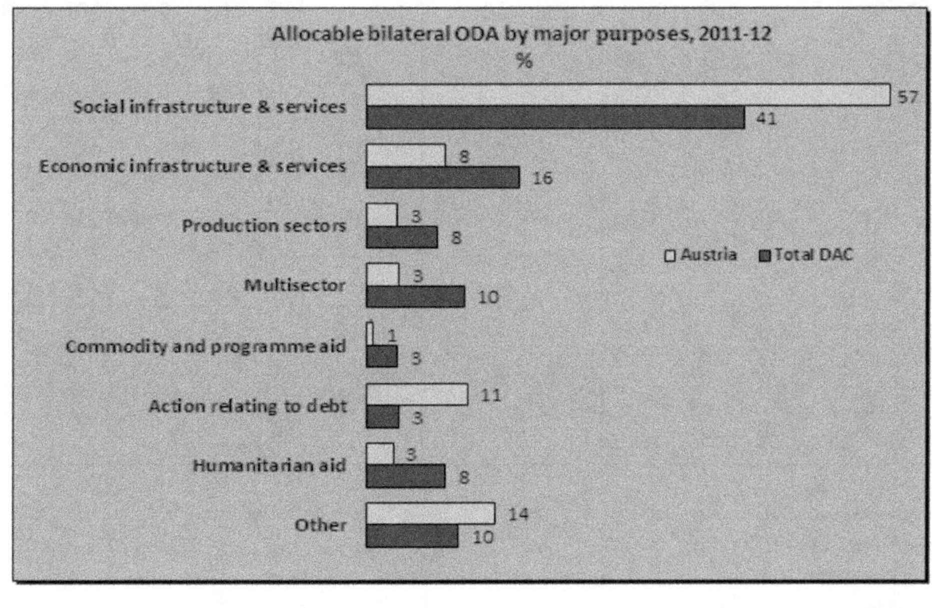

Table B.6 Comparative aid performance

Net disbursements

	Official development assistance			Grant element of ODA (commitments)	Share of multilateral aid				ODA to LDCs Bilateral and through multilateral agencies	
	2012		2006-07 to 2011-12 Average annual % change in real terms	2012	2012				2012	
	USD million	% of GNI		% (a)	% of ODA (b)	% of ODA (c)	% of GNI (b)	% of GNI (c)	% of ODA	% of GNI
Australia	5 403	0.36	7.1	99.8	15.8		0.06		30.3	0.11
Austria	1 106	0.28	-9.5	100.0	51.6	26.7	0.14	0.07	22.0	0.06
Belgium	2 315	0.47	3.0	99.7	38.1	18.7	0.18	0.09	30.4	0.14
Canada	5 650	0.32	3.2	100.0	28.3		0.09		34.4	0.11
Czech Republic	220	0.12	2.9	100.0	69.8	16.2	0.08	0.02	26.7	0.03
Denmark	2 693	0.83	0.4	100.0	28.6	19.7	0.24	0.16	37.3	0.31
Finland	1 320	0.53	5.9	100.0	39.5	25.3	0.21	0.13	33.7	0.18
France	12 028	0.45	2.0	79.5	34.1	16.7	0.15	0.08	21.1	0.10
Germany	12 939	0.37	2.0	88.4	33.7	14.9	0.13	0.06	28.4	0.11
Greece	327	0.13	-6.4	100.0	67.2	4.9	0.09	0.01	15.3	0.02
Iceland	26	0.22	-5.7	100.0	18.8		0.04		45.1	0.10
Ireland	808	0.47	-4.0	100.0	33.7	17.9	0.16	0.08	51.7	0.24
Italy	2 737	0.14	-3.6	99.4	77.2	21.8	0.11	0.03	25.6	0.04
Japan	10 605	0.17	-3.6	88.5	39.6		0.07		43.8	0.08
Korea	1 597	0.14	21.6	94.2	25.9		0.04		36.2	0.05
Luxembourg	399	1.00	0.5	100.0	30.7	22.8	0.31	0.23	36.5	0.37
Netherlands	5 523	0.71	-1.2	100.0	30.2	19.2	0.21	0.14	21.1	0.15
New Zealand	449	0.28	3.0	100.0	19.5		0.05		32.0	0.09
Norway	4 753	0.93	1.7	100.0	25.9		0.24		29.1	0.27
Poland	421	0.09	3.1	..	73.5	5.8	0.07	0.01	18.5	0.02
Portugal	581	0.28	6.8	84.6	31.6	5.1	0.09	0.01	30.4	0.09
Slovak Republic	80	0.09	1.5	100.0	76.2	8.3	0.07	0.01	19.3	0.02
Slovenia	58	0.13	2.0	100.0	67.3	13.8	0.09	0.02	17.3	0.02
Spain	2 037	0.16	-8.3	100.0	51.6	4.6	0.08	0.01	23.7	0.04
Sweden	5 240	0.97	2.3	100.0	30.6	24.0	0.30	0.23	29.4	0.29
Switzerland	3 056	0.47	5.5	100.0	19.6		0.09		23.2	0.11
United Kingdom	13 891	0.56	5.5	100.0	37.3	23.9	0.21	0.13	33.2	0.19
United States	30 687	0.19	4.6	100.0	17.0		0.03		37.2	0.07
Total DAC	126 949	0.29	2.0	94.6	30.2		0.09		31.9	0.09
Memo: Average country effort		0.39								

Notes:

a. Excluding debt reorganisation.

b. Including EU institutions.

c. Excluding EU institutions.

.. Data not available.

Figure B.1 Net ODA from DAC countries in 2012

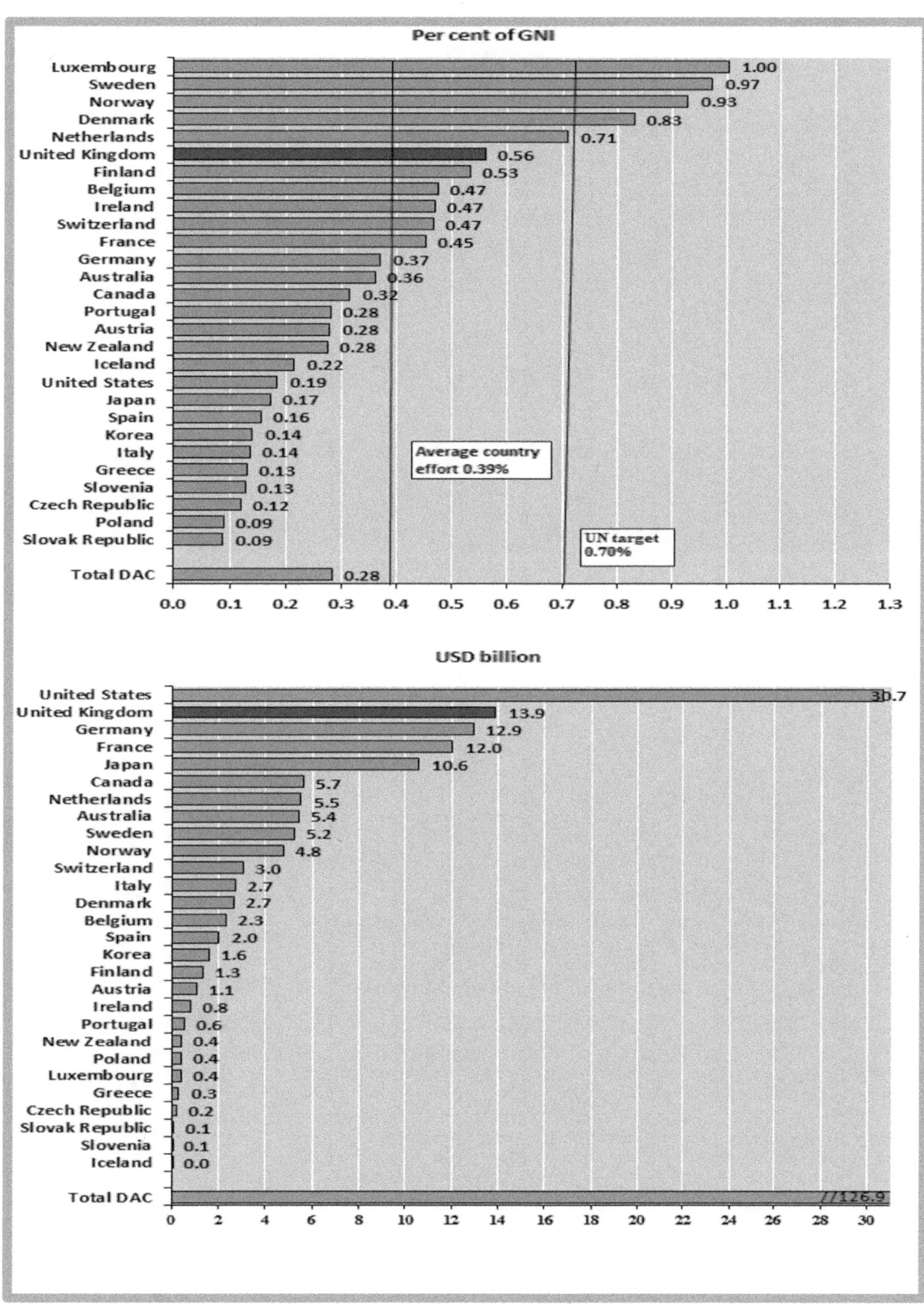

Annex C: Field visit to Moldova

A team of examiners and the OECD Secretariat visited Moldova in June 2014 as part of the peer review of Austria. The team met Austrian development professionals, partner country civil servants, other bilateral and multilateral partners, and representatives of Austrian and partner country civil society organisations, the private sector, and local and regional authorities as well as parliamentarians.

Context[1]

Moldova is a lower middle-income country, with a population of 3.6 million and a gross domestic product (GDP) per capita of USD 3 368 (2012).[2] It depends heavily on remittances (estimated at USD 1 billion annually) from the estimated 1 million Moldovans working in the EU or in the Russian Federation (hereafter "Russia") and other countries. Moldova is one of the EU's Eastern Partnership initiative countries. The association and free-trade agreement with the EU was initialled in November 2013 (with the final text to be signed in September 2014). The government's primary goal of EU integration has resulted in some market-oriented progress, and the granting of EU trade preferences has encouraged high growth rates.

Moldova's economy has recovered from the 2008-09 global financial crisis, with average annual GDP growth exceeding 5% in 2010-13. The national poverty and extreme poverty rates fell from 30.2% and 4.5%, respectively, in 2006 to 16.6% and 0.6% in 2012, making Moldova one of the world's top performers with respect to poverty reduction. Nevertheless, Moldova remains one of the poorest countries in Europe. It ranks low on the Human Development Index (HDI): out of 187 countries and territories, it was 114th in 2013 (UNDP, 2014). There is also a frozen conflict within its borders in the region of Transnistria.[3] Moldova's economic future remains vulnerable to political uncertainty, weak administrative capacity, corruption, higher fuel prices[4] and the concerns of foreign investors.[5] With Russia committed to resisting increased EU influence in the region, tension and instability could increase in Moldova.[6]

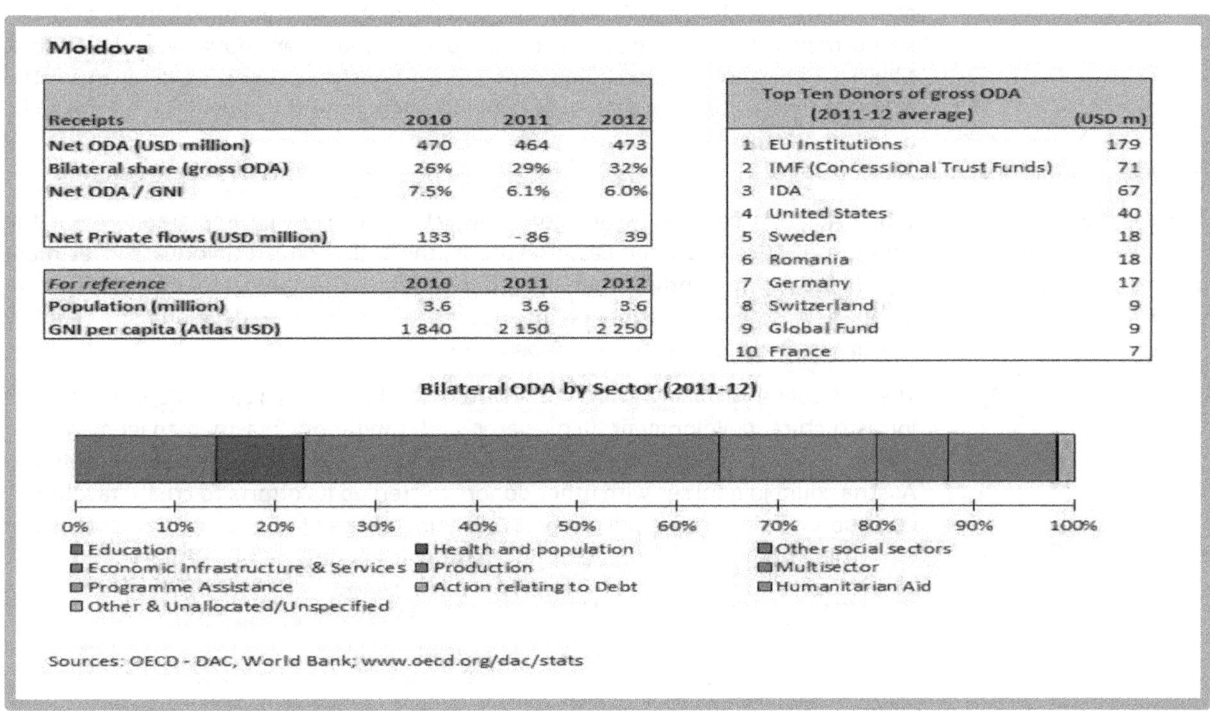

Moldova

Receipts	2010	2011	2012
Net ODA (USD million)	470	464	473
Bilateral share (gross ODA)	26%	29%	32%
Net ODA / GNI	7.5%	6.1%	6.0%
Net Private flows (USD million)	133	- 86	39

For reference	2010	2011	2012
Population (million)	3.6	3.6	3.6
GNI per capita (Atlas USD)	1 840	2 150	2 250

	Top Ten Donors of gross ODA (2011-12 average)	(USD m)
1	EU Institutions	179
2	IMF (Concessional Trust Funds)	71
3	IDA	67
4	United States	40
5	Sweden	18
6	Romania	18
7	Germany	17
8	Switzerland	9
9	Global Fund	9
10	France	7

Bilateral ODA by Sector (2011-12)

Sources: OECD - DAC, World Bank; www.oecd.org/dac/stats

Towards a comprehensive Austrian development effort

Austria's programme is coherent with its foreign policy objectives

Geographical proximity and historical ties contribute to making Moldova a priority country for Austrian Development Cooperation (ADC). Austria's political commitment in Moldova reflects its broader strategy in the Danube Region/Western Balkans aimed at supporting the EU's Eastern Partnership Initiative. Thus, Austria is implementing its foreign policy objectives, focusing on ensuring security in the region, as well as its development objectives for Moldova's socio-economic progress.

A whole-of-government approach is lacking

Austria's Country Strategy for Moldova 2011-2015 (MFA, 2010) is not designed as a whole-of-government approach. The ADC co-ordination office's work plan for Moldova only covers activities that the Austrian Development Agency (ADA) directly administers. There is no formalised system for co-ordinating the activities of all the different Austrian stakeholders involved. Informal communication between ADC and the other federal ministries seems to be working, however.[7] The head of the ADC office solicits the expertise of the line ministry attachés and consultants in response to specific needs and organises meetings with these actors every two months on average. The ADC office also co-operates closely with the trade attaché based at the embassy in Bucharest on the Business Partnership Programme.

A coherent approach at country level is difficult, however, without a whole-of-government approach. The fact that the corporate brand "ADC" is not used by other official Austrian actors is symptomatic of this challenge. The Federal Ministry of Education and Women's Affairs, for example, has a separate co-operation agreement (a memorandum of understanding) with Moldova and implements its own projects. There is scope for strengthening the head of the ADC office's role as co-ordinator of all official Austrian aid, and for more structured exchanges between all Austrian actors, including those not represented in Moldova (e.g. the Federal Ministry of Science, Research and Economy and Austria's export credit agency). The ADC Country Strategy for Moldova should also integrate the activities undertaken by different line ministries.

There is scope to use ODA as a catalyst for private sector-led development

While Austrian companies are generally active in investing and trading with the countries in South-East and Eastern Europe, the scale of Austrian private investment in Moldova is currently rather limited.[8] Austria is beginning to explore ways to increase Austrian investments in support of Moldova's development, namely through its Business Partnership Programme.

There is scope for using grants to leverage credits on a larger scale in support of infrastructure development (e.g. water and sanitation, waste management and energy) and for setting conditions for additional Austrian investments in Moldova. Austria could join forces with other donors to step up its efforts to create favourable conditions for increasing private flows.[9] Signing of the EU Deep and Comprehensive Free Trade Area agreement is a positive strategic initiative in this respect.

Austria's policies, strategies and aid allocations

Austria aligns to Moldova's development priorities

Austria's bilateral co-operation programme in Moldova began in 2001. Since 2004 Moldova has also been one of ADC's remaining three priority countries in South-Eastern and Eastern Europe. Austria is a pragmatic, predictable and trusted partner for Moldova, capable of adapting its assistance to changing circumstances and to the country's specific needs. It is an active and appreciated EU member and a strong supporter of Moldova's efforts to achieve European integration. Austria considers that Moldova deserves a "clear European perspective" (MFA, 2010).

The Three-Year Programme on Austrian Development Policy 2013-2015 (MFA, 2012) and the Country Strategy for Moldova 2011-2015 (MFA, 2010) constitute the basis of Austria's bilateral co-operation policy. Its support is consistent with the EU's European Neighbourhood Policy and aligns closely to the priorities of the Moldova 2020: the National Development Strategy (Government of Republic of Moldova, 2012) and the EU-Moldova Action Plan (EC, 2005). Poverty reduction is a central concern and an overarching goal of ADC. The Country Strategy identifies two priority areas for its bilateral co-operation: i) social infrastructure, particularly water and waste water management in rural areas; and ii) labour market oriented vocational education and training. Building on its long and successful tradition of working on water supply and vocational training, the ADC's programmes aim at contributing to the MDGs, particularly Target 1B (achieve full and productive employment and decent work for all, including women and young people) and Target 7C (to halve, by 2015, the proportion of people with sustainable access to safe drinking water and basic sanitation).

The ADC's small but focused programme attempts to strike a balance between a poverty focus and foreign policy considerations (e.g. peace, security and the territorial integrity of Moldova linked to the Transnistria conflict), business, and environmentally sustainable development. In the area of water and sanitation, ADC works with local municipalities and civil society to contribute to implementing Moldova's National Water Supply and Sanitation Sector Strategy (2007, 2014) aimed at improving access to safe drinking water and sanitation by rural populations. The ADC also contributes to the creation of a modern vocational training system capable of being adapted to the needs of a competitive labour market, in line with Moldova's National Vocational Education and Training Development Strategy (2013) and its National Education Strategy (2014).[10] Austria looks for synergies and linkages, particularly in regard to water and sanitation, where it combines its activities with others related to climate change adaptation, gender equality and vocational training. Its approach to poverty reduction is well illustrated by its support targeting the poorest municipalities in the central western region of Moldova, as well as training activities targeting disadvantaged groups.

Other areas of ADC intervention include governance (including strengthening the rule of law and human rights), migration management, strengthening civil society, agriculture, health, and gender equality and women's empowerment. Austria puts particular emphasis on governance in its support to civil society and municipalities along the two banks of the Dniester River, as a contribution to resolution of the Transnistria conflict. In doing so it works with the Organization for Security and Co-operation in Europe (OSCE), the EU and the Council of Europe.

Austria is Moldova's ninth largest donor

While Moldova is not an overly aid-dependent country, its per capita ODA level is high at USD 132. ODA to Moldova more than tripled between 2004 and 2012, reaching USD 473 million in 2012 and making up 6% of the country's national income. The EU is by far the biggest provider of ODA to Moldova, providing USD 178.8 million on average between 2011 and 2012.

Austria provided USD 3.9 million, on average, as net ODA between 2011 and 2012, making it Moldova's ninth largest donor. Between 2004 and 2012, Austria provided a cumulative total of EUR 22.3 million in ODA to the country. According to the Austrian federal government, EUR 1.9 million has been earmarked for bilateral ODA to Moldova for 2014.

Austria's support mainly focuses on its two priority sectors (water supply and sanitation, and vocational education and training), with a particular emphasis on governance as a cross-cutting issue (Figure C.1). Comparing the budget scenario included in the Country Strategy with actual spending in 2013, however, the target of allocating 90% to the two priority sectors does not appear to have been respected.

In addition to grant support, a framework agreement was signed between Moldova and Austria (the Federal Ministry of Finance and Austria's export credit agency) in 2012. Austria has allocated EUR 7.5 million (2013-14) and another EUR 7.2 million (2014-15) towards improving health care services at the Republican Hospital of Moldova.

The ADC co-ordination office also directly funds small projects, such as developing a short-term training course in rural tourism and an advanced distance learning course in the Romanian language for national minorities. It has also funded an environmental education programme to promote awareness of river basin protection.

Figure C.1 Austria's bilateral ODA to Moldova by sector, gross disbursements, 2011-12 average

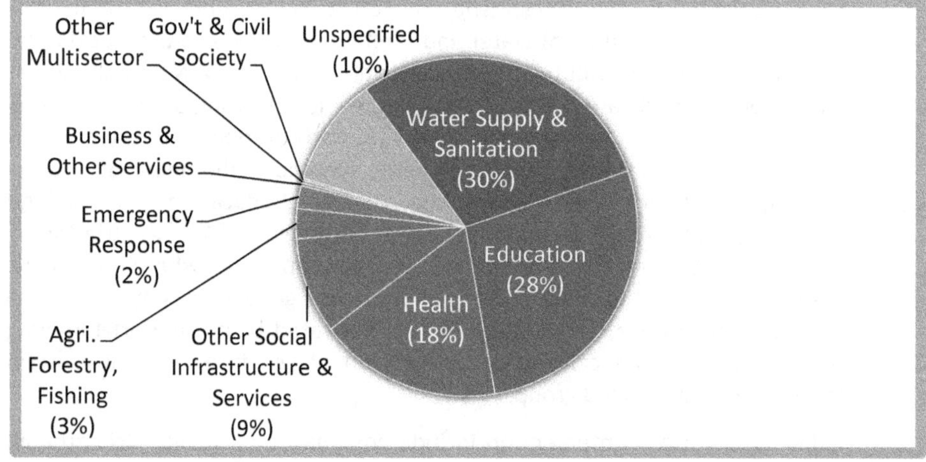

More support and guidance from headquarters is needed to mainstream gender equality

Moldova performs well in some areas of gender equality, yet disparities persist in education, health, economic opportunity, and violence against women. Austria conducts a number of gender-focused and environment-related activities, mostly through local partners and Austrian NGOs. Gender equality and the environment are mainstreamed in the area of water and sanitation, and included in the results matrix of the Country Strategy. However, the Country Strategy does not have verifiable indicators. The ADC co-ordination office has no designated focal points or specific budgets for mainstreaming these themes into its programmes, and relevant tools and procedures (e.g. a gender action plan, procedures for reporting on results and accountability mechanisms) are also lacking.

Further gender training of ADC local staff, targeting their specific needs, as well as more support from headquarters with appropriate tools and procedures, would contribute to strengthening this aspect of the programme.

Organisation and management

Delegation of political authority to the head of ADC is positive

The Austrian Development Agency (ADA) opened a co-ordination office for technical co-operation in Chisinau in 2005. It was upgraded to an embassy in 2007. The resident Ambassador in Bucharest, Romania, concurrently serves as Ambassador to Moldova, with the head of the ADC co-ordination office[11] in Chisinau accredited as attaché for development co-operation. The head of the ADC office reports to Bucharest or jointly with Bucharest to Vienna on all political matters, although on urgent matters the head of the ADC office has reported directly to Vienna in close co-ordination with Bucharest. This contributes to enhancing Austria's visibility and its role in Moldova, and helps strengthen the links between Austria's development co-operation and foreign policy objectives.

The ADC co-ordination office administers the co-operation programme with support from the ADA's Quality Assurance and Knowledge Management Division, the NGO Co-operation Division, and the Finance and Audit Division. The co-ordination office produces two yearly reports for the ADA's headquarters and the MFA. Relations with the MFA focus more on programming. Communication flows between the ADC co-ordination office, the embassy in Bucharest, the ADA headquarters and the MFA appear to be fluid. They could be facilitated with improved technology (e.g. intranet).

ADC's human resources are well suited to the size and scope of Austria's programme

Austria's small team of development professionals is well suited to the size and scope of its programme in Moldova. The head of the ADC co-ordination office manages four locally recruited ADA staff members (two sector advisors on water and sanitation and on professional education, one administrative staff member and one driver). In addition, three embassy attachés deployed from the ministries of social affairs, education and the interior report to their respective ministries in Vienna. The head of the ADC office has protocol-related responsibility over the attachés.

Local staff members are highly valued. Their expertise, country knowledge and experience contribute to Austria's ability to respond to field imperatives. They also facilitate engagement with local communities of practice. The ADC does not have a specific human resource policy with respect to locally recruited staff. The conditions of employment depend on Moldova's legislation. The ADC office has an annual budget of EUR 2 000 for training purposes, either at ADA's headquarters or, more frequently, in the region.

Partnerships, results and accountability

A project-based approach, implemented by a variety of partners

ADC's projects financed through grants are implemented by a variety of partners (e.g. national and local government institutions, NGOs, trade unions, academia and research institutes, international organisations and private firms). To foster local ownership and participation, Austria makes increasing use of local capacities and expertise in regard to project identification and implementation.[12] It also uses national data and indicators to the extent possible when monitoring and assessing its programmes. ADC supports civil society activities and forms partnerships with local NGOs through a specific co-financing instrument. Proposals are to be submitted by Austrian NGOs in co-operation with a local partner in the framework of the call for proposals. The EU co-financing instrument supports projects by Austrian NGOs that are co-financed by ADC and the European Commission.

Moldova is a focus country for the EU Fast Track Initiative of Division of Labour. Austria actively supports and engages in donor co-ordination, including through delegated co-operation and silent partnerships, to increase the alignment of EU assistance, leveraging resources in addressing critical gaps while avoiding overlaps. Austria co-funds (through a silent partnership) the Swiss Agency for Development and Cooperation (SDC)-led project on sanitation (the ApaSan project) and co-ordinates its activities with the World Bank and the European Bank for Reconstruction and Development (EBRD). In 2008 Austria signed a memorandum of understanding with the Czech Development Agency to strengthen partnerships in the water sector. Austria shares its on-going and planned project information with other EU member states and contributes to the EU aid co-ordination matrix (managed and facilitated by the EU delegation in Chisinau). It also provides timely information on its aid flows to the Moldovan government through the new Aid Management Platform.

Austria is fully committed to EU joint programming and implements an EU Delegation Agreement in Moldova. The ADA has the lead in implementing an EU programme providing safe drinking water to the Nisporeni district (population of around 23 000) in the framework of indirect centralised management, co-financed by the EU (EUR 5 million) and the SDC (EUR 0.8 million). Austria also co-operates on and co-funds vocational education and training projects with Lichtenstein, its main strategic donor partner for this sector. The ADC co-ordination office endeavours to target Austria's multi-bi contributions with a view to developing synergies with its bilateral activities. Austria also actively works with the UN in Moldova, namely with the UN Industrial Development Organisation (UNIDO) on the National Cleaner Production Programme and on Regional Networking for Strengthening Cooperation and Fostering Transfer and Adaptation of Resource Efficient and Cleaner Production in the countries of South-Eastern Europe.

Box C.1 Donor co-ordination mechanisms in Moldova

The State Chancellery is designated as the National Aid Co-ordination Authority by Government Decision No. 12 (dated 19 January 2010) and is responsible for the co-ordination of programming, monitoring and evaluation of all external aid flows to Moldova. Its responsibilities include: i) provision of support to the relevant public administration institutions in improving the sector external assistance co-ordination mechanism; ii) monitoring and evaluation of external assistance to maximise its impact on the economic development of the country; and iii) ensuring transparency of external assistance and the implementation of a communications policy with the donor community and civil society.

There are about 30 bilateral and multilateral donors active in Moldova. The Partnership Principles Implementation Plan, signed in March 2010 between the government and its key development partners (the World Bank, the EU, the UN and bilateral donors), lays out the principles of international co-operation. To ensure alignment of Moldova's EU commitments with the goals set out in the partnership plan, the EU Fast-Track Initiative of Division of Labour and the "European dimension" were incorporated into the plan. The State Chancellery has also established a network of Sector Co-ordination Councils to manage and monitor the effectiveness of external assistance in priority sectors.

In the area of environment, the Donor Co-ordination Council, headed by the Minister of the Environment, convenes regularly with all relevant donors: ADC, the EU, EBRD, SDC, the Turkish International Cooperation and Coordination Agency (TIKA), the World Bank and others. Regular donor co-ordination meetings, chaired by the Minister of Education, ensure co-ordination and harmonisation in VET with all relevant donors (currently ADC, Liechtenstein, GIZ and UNICEF). In the water sector, the European Water Initiative through the OECD's Environmental Action Programme Taskforce has established a structured National Policy Dialogue since 2006 for financing water supply. The dialogue involves all major government and civil society stakeholders and is led by the Ministry of Environment.

Moldova is using development co-operation to focus on domestic resource mobilisation, increase transparency in donor interactions and prevent work duplication. It is also using several measures to manage the aid it receives effectively, increase its ownership, enhance transparency, and ensure donors back up their promises with actions. Most recently, the government launched a new online Aid Management Platform in January 2014 to allow public access to project information, commitments and plans, and to bolster transparency and co-ordination among the private sector, government, donors and civil society. The government's BOOST platform provides access to national budget and public expenditure information. Its "Date.gov.md" website, launched in April 2011, goes even further – making 725 sets of government data from 39 central public authorities fully available to public scrutiny. These are all important elements that strengthen mutual accountability and contribute to the realisation of inclusive participation, including by civil society, business, the media and the public.

Challenges remain, however. There are significant gaps in the use of country systems (e.g. outcome frameworks, budgeting elements, reporting, auditing procedures and acquisition procedures) by Moldova's external partners. This is despite some of national systems having been recognised by the World Bank's Country Policy and Institutional Assessment, and the Public Expenditure and Financial Accountability Framework, as high quality.

Source: State Chancellery of the Republic of Moldova (2013), MFA (2010).

Austria is a predictable partner; more effort is needed in the use of country systems

Although ADC's budget for Moldova is relatively stable, the aid predictability of the overall Austrian budget is limited given that it does not include funding from all ministries. An overall budget framework, including funding from all Austrian actors, would make Austria's budget more predictable for Moldova.

Austria delivers some aspects of its water supply programme using local procurement. In line with its Busan commitment, Austria could work with the government and other external stakeholders to strengthen Moldova's national systems.

The ADC office manages risks, but more support and guidance from headquarters are needed

How major risks to the success of the overall development portfolio are identified, analysed, managed or monitored is not clear. While Austria takes a sufficiently systematic approach to risks in its activities in the breakaway region of Transnistria, the ADC co-ordination office does not appear to receive sufficient guidance from Vienna to take a comprehensive approach to risks throughout the country programme. Staff are left to decide the best ways to incorporate risk management into programming. A specific section on risk management in the Country Strategy for the whole programme would be useful.

NGOs are key strategic partners

Austria promotes ownership at the national and sub-national levels, and co-operates closely with local institutions and stakeholders. Financing of, and engagement with, Moldovan grassroots organisations and NGOs are important aspects of its programme. However, transaction costs appear to be high relative to available funding. There is scope for reducing and simplifying administrative requirements, as well as procedures for funding and reporting. Encouraging local NGOs to network among themselves and with other stakeholders would benefit these organisations.

Efforts are made to strengthen the focus on results and learning

Austria is beginning to strengthen the result orientation of its country programme, relying on country data where available. Its monitoring and evaluation practices appear to be robust at the project level. The Country Strategy includes a results framework. Efforts are made to relate project results to strategic development goals and verifiable indicators in the two priority sectors, and to monitor these results. The indicators are taken from the framework elaborated by the EU in the area of water and sanitation; they are linked to ADC's vocational training project portfolio. The indicators for cross-cutting issues are mainly qualitative, and there are no indicators for non-priority sectors.

Austria is encouraged to pursue its efforts to link projects' indicators to the country strategy and to national goals. It would gain from integrating indicators related to cross-cutting issues in priority sectors, and from relating results assessments more strongly to periodic reporting. The future country programme would benefit from an evaluation, with the recommendations serving as the basis for crafting the next programme.

Austria has begun to use good and bad practices as a basis for learning in the water and sanitation sector. Building on this, it could develop an approach to institutional learning by documenting good and bad practices more systematically and reporting these practices to headquarters on a regular basis. In that context, Austria could seek inputs from external stakeholders (e.g. other donors, research institutes and academia). The ADC co-ordination office's support to Moldova-based NGOs, in the context of following up on evaluation recommendations, contributes to learning within these organisations. These efforts can be built on to strengthen learning and knowledge management throughout the programme.

Notes

1. Sources: EIU, 2014; MFA, 2010; OECD/DAC statistics.

2. Source: The World Bank's World Development Indicators (http://data.worldbank.org/data-catalog/world-development-indicators).

3. Although Moldova gained its independence following the breakup of the Soviet Union in 1991, Russian forces have remained on Moldovan territory east of the Dniester River supporting the separatist Transnistria region. The break-away state of Transnistria is a Russian-speaking enclave within Moldova composed of a Slavic majority population (mostly Ukrainians and Russians) but with a sizeable ethnic Moldovan minority. Transnistria claims to have seceded and to have established an independent country. The Organization for Security and Co-operation in Europe (OSCE) is trying to facilitate a negotiated settlement between Moldova and Transnistria, and the region remains under the auspices of an OSCE-mandated peacekeeping mission comprising Moldovan, Transnistrian, Russian and Ukrainian troops.

4. Moldova imports almost all its energy supplies from Russia.

5. Growth has been hampered by Russian import bans on Moldovan wine and agricultural products, high prices for Russian natural gas, and Moldova's large debt.

6. Russia's attitude to Moldova has hardened in recent years. It has been trying to halt Moldova's EU integration by imposing sanctions such as the suspension of wine imports from Moldova, and has even threatened to cut off the gas supplies on which Moldovans depend. These developments represent potentially grave risks to Moldova's economic and political stability in the coming months.

7. There are examples of inter-ministerial co-operation. The Federal Ministry of Labour, Social Affairs and Consumer Protection works with the ADC co-ordination office to implement labour market-oriented professional education and social projects. The Federal Ministry of the Interior implements activities funded by ADA. The ADA is implementing a climate change project funded by the Federal Ministry of Agriculture, Forestry, Environment and Water Management. The ADC co-ordination office was tasked to support and monitor implementation of soft loan projects financed by the Federal Ministry of Finance in the health sector.

8. The review team was informed that only about a dozen Austrian companies were actively investing in Moldova at the time of its visit.

9. This view was shared by the private sector representatives the review team met in Moldova.

10. Austria has also deployed two advisors to the Moldovan Ministry of Education to support the Ministry's efforts with respect to the reform of the national vocational education and training system.

11. The head of the ADC co-ordination office is recruited by the ADA and appointed by the Minister of Foreign Affairs.

12. For example, Austria's projects related to vocational training engage the private sector, pilot schools and the Moldovan Ministry of Education in policy dialogue.

Bibliography

Government sources

MFA (Austrian Federal Ministry for Europe, Integration and Foreign Affairs) (2010), *Moldova: Country Strategy 2011-2015*, MFA, Vienna, www.entwicklung.at/uploads/media/CS_Moldau_2011-2015_01.pdf.

Government of Republic of Moldova (2012), *Moldova 2020 – National Development Strategy: 7 Solutions for Economic Growth and Poverty Reduction*, State Chancellery, Chisinau, www.gov.md/public/files/Moldova_2020_ENG.pdf.

State Chancellery of the Republic of Moldova (2013), *Development Cooperation: 2012 Annual Report on External Assistance Provided to the Republic of Moldova*, State Chancellery, Chisinau, www.ncu.moldova.md/public/files/AE_REPORT_2012_eng.pdf.

Other sources

EC (European Commission) (2005), *EU-Moldova Action Plan*, an ENPI project, EC, Brussels, www.enpi-info.eu/library/content/eu-moldova-action-plan.

EIU (Economist Intelligence Unit) (2014), *Country Report: Moldova*, 1st Quarter 2014, EIU, London, http://country.eiu.com/moldova.

UNDP (United Nations Development Programme) (2014), *Human Development Report 2014. Sustaining Human Progress: Reducing Vulnerabilities and Building Resilience*, UNDP, New York, http://hdr.undp.org/en/2014-report.

Annex D: Organisational structure

Human Resource Profile

				2009	2013
Institution	Type of staff			No. of posts filled	No. of posts filled
MFA	Experts and diplomats			21	22
	Trainees			2	3
	Support			10	8
ADA	Experts	Headquarters (HQ)		87	83
		Field offices	From HQ	23	16
			Locally recruited	52	45
		Other missions		-	2
MoF	Financial experts	HQ		10	10
		Representation at IFIs		6	5
Austrian Development Bank	Experts (e.g. financial, legal, risk)			11	29
	Support			2	3
Total				224	226

Organisational Chart 1 - Federal Ministry for Europe, Integration and Foreign Affairs (MFA), Directorate-General for Development Cooperation (April 2014)

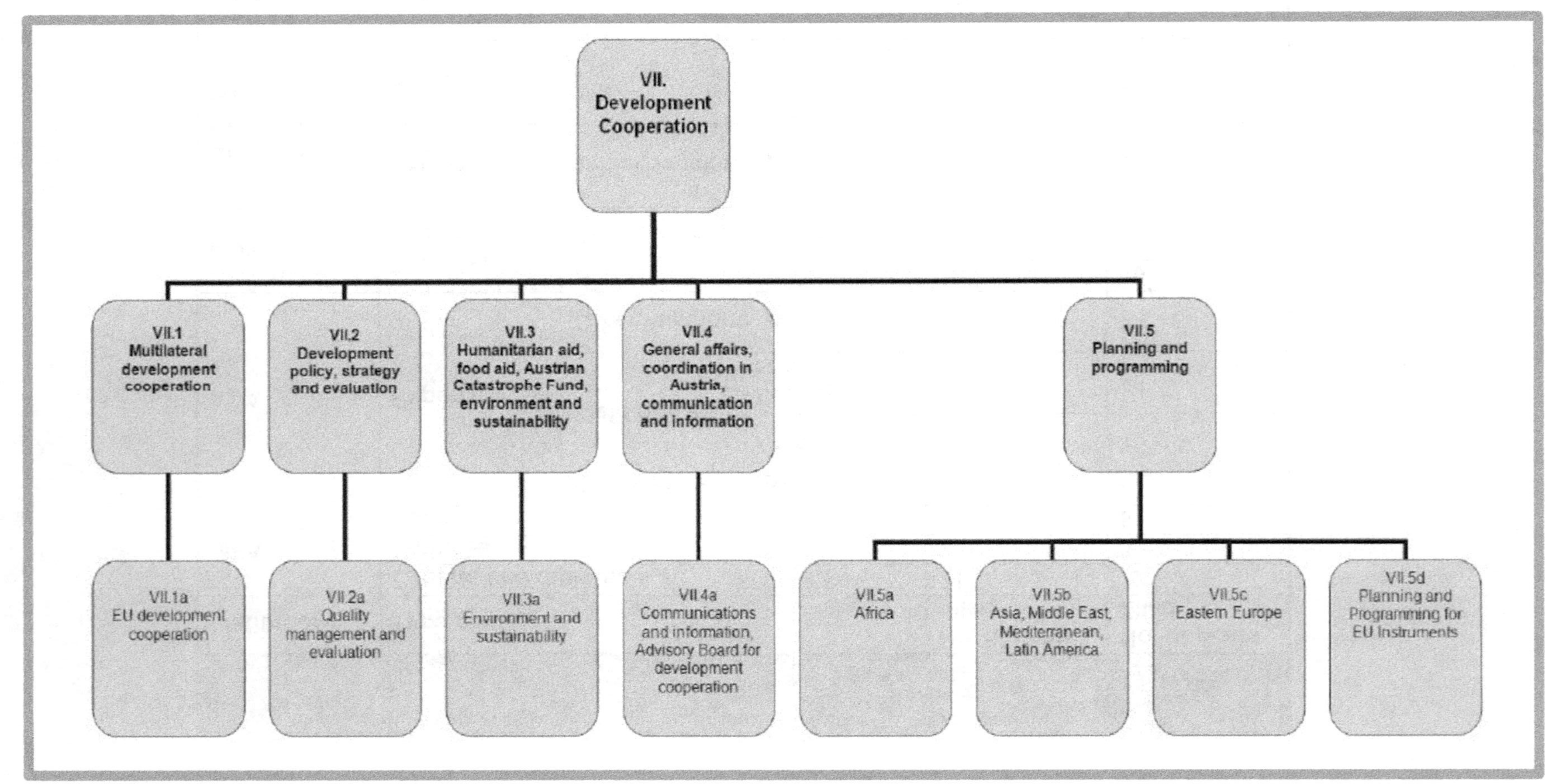

Organisational Chart 2 - Austrian Development Agency (ADA)

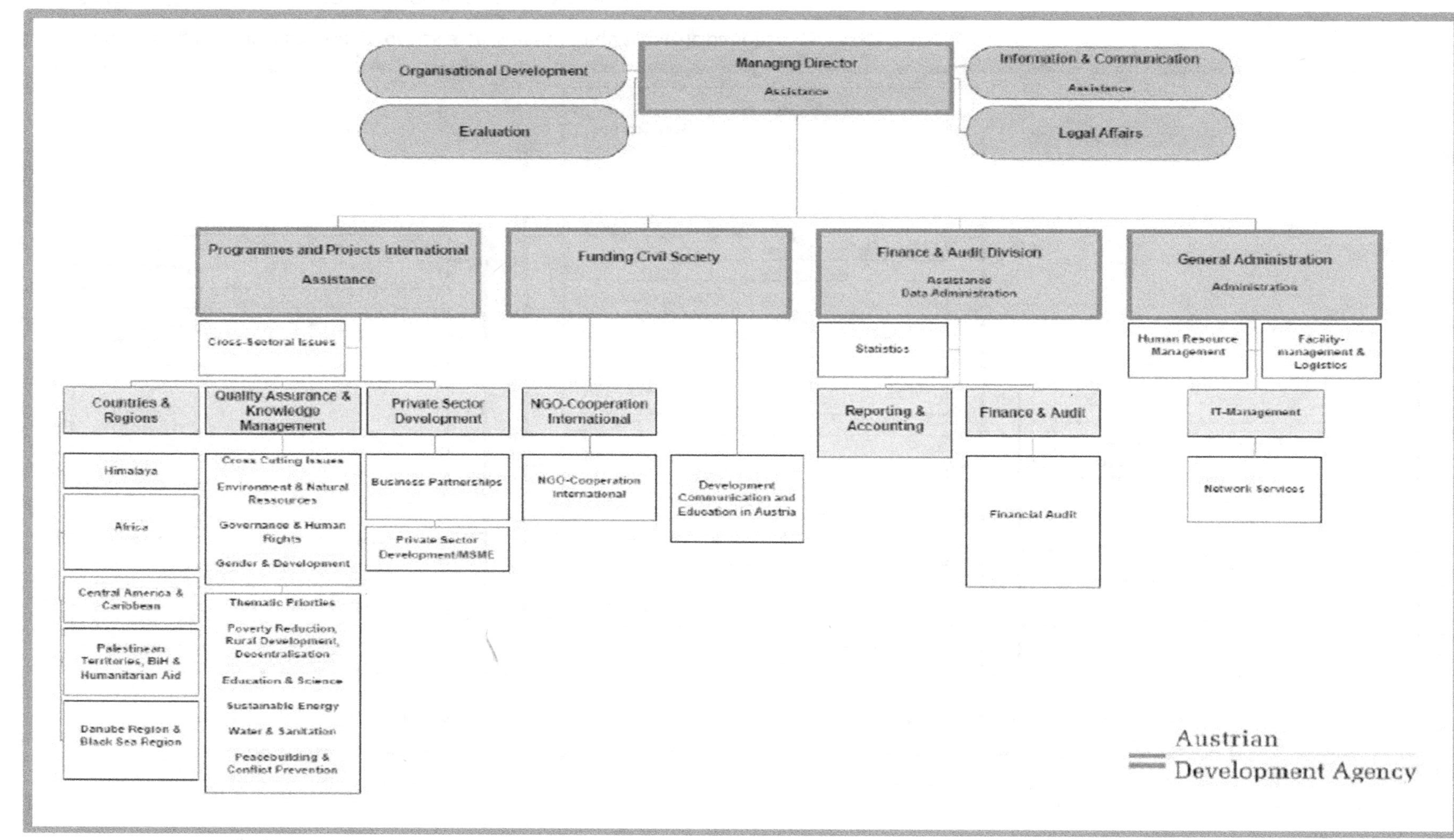

Organisational Chart 3 - Austrian Development Bank

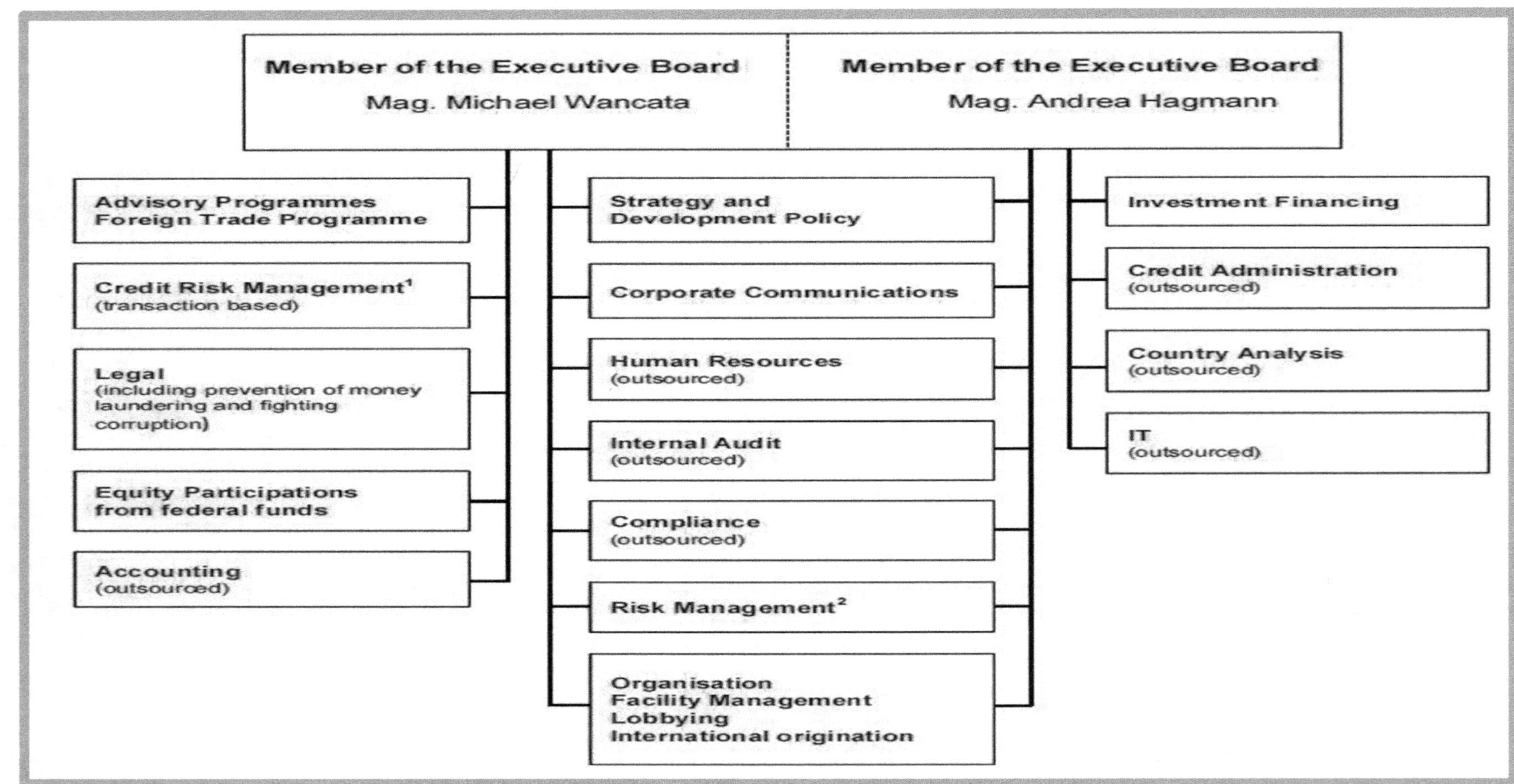

1. Andrea Hagmann is responsible for risk assessment of equity participations.
2. Michael Wancata is responsible for operational implementation.

ORGANISATION FOR ECONOMIC CO-OPERATION AND DEVELOPMENT

The OECD is a unique forum where governments work together to address the economic, social and environmental challenges of globalisation. The OECD is also at the forefront of efforts to understand and to help governments respond to new developments and concerns, such as corporate governance, the information economy and the challenges of an ageing population. The Organisation provides a setting where governments can compare policy experiences, seek answers to common problems, identify good practice and work to co-ordinate domestic and international policies.

The OECD member countries are: Australia, Austria, Belgium, Canada, Chile, the Czech Republic, Denmark, Estonia, Finland, France, Germany, Greece, Hungary, Iceland, Ireland, Israel, Italy, Japan, Korea, Luxembourg, Mexico, the Netherlands, New Zealand, Norway, Poland, Portugal, the Slovak Republic, Slovenia, Spain, Sweden, Switzerland, Turkey, the United Kingdom and the United States. The European Union takes part in the work of the OECD.

OECD Publishing disseminates widely the results of the Organisation's statistics gathering and research on economic, social and environmental issues, as well as the conventions, guidelines and standards agreed by its members.

DEVELOPMENT ASSISTANCE COMMITTEE

To achieve its aims, the OECD has set up a number of specialised committees. One of these is the Development Assistance Committee (DAC), whose mandate is to promote development co-operation and other policies so as to contribute to sustainable development – including pro-poor economic growth, poverty reduction and the improvement of living standards in developing countries – and to a future in which no country will depend on aid. To this end, the DAC has grouped the world's main donors, defining and monitoring global standards in key areas of development.

The members of the DAC are Australia, Austria, Belgium, Canada, the Czech Republic, Denmark, the European Union, Finland, France, Germany, Greece, Iceland, Ireland, Italy, Japan, Korea, Luxembourg, the Netherlands, New Zealand, Norway, Poland, Portugal, the Slovak Republic, Slovenia, Spain, Sweden, Switzerland, the United Kingdom and the United States.

The DAC issues guidelines and reference documents in the DAC Guidelines and Reference Series to inform and assist members in the conduct of their development co-operation programmes.

OECD PUBLISHING, 2, rue André-Pascal, 75775 PARIS CEDEX 16
(43 2014 13 1 P) ISBN 978-92-64-22794-1 – 2015-07

www.ingramcontent.com/pod-product-compliance
Lightning Source LLC
LaVergne TN
LVHW081412110826
845149LV00010B/1718